GREECE

A Travellers' Guide

D1431644

GREECE

A Traveller's Guide

ELISABETH DE STROUMILLO

HIPPOCRENE
BOOKS, INC.

Distribution:
Distributed in Great Britain and the Commonwealth by
Roger Lascelles, 47 York Road, Brentford, Middlesex TW8 0QP
Telephone: 01-847-0935

ISBN 0 902726 45 5

Distributed in the United States and Canada by
Hippocrene Books Inc., 171 Madison Avenue, New York NY 10016

US ISBN 0 87052 718 5

Published by Thornton Cox (1986) Ltd,
Epworth House, 23-35 City Road, London EC1 1AA

Published in the United States and Canada by
Hippocrene Books Inc., 171 Madison Avenue, New York, NY 10016

First published by Thornton Cox Ltd, 1974
Second edition published by Geographia Ltd, 1980
This edition, fully revised, 1989

Drawings by William McLaren
Maps by Tom Stalker-Miller, MSIA
Series Editor: Kit Harding

Cover: Entrance to the Acropolis, Athens. Photograph Elisabeth de Stroumillo.

Inside colour photographs by Elisabeth de Stroumillo with the exception
of: Kapnikarea Church (page 34), Samothraki (page 101), Santorini (page
103), Kavala (page 103), Street Scene (page 104) by courtesy Greek
National Tourist Office, and Ios (page 104) Hutchison Library.

*Great care has been taken throughout this book to be accurate, but
the publishers cannot accept responsibility for any errors which appear*

Printed in Great Britain by The Guernsey Press Company Limited,
Guernsey, Channel Islands. Set in 8½ on 9½ pt Univers

Thornton Cox Guides:

Titles in print in this series include:

Egypt	**Majorca**
Ireland	**Portugal**
Kenya	**Southern France**

The Acropolis, Athens

Contents

Author's Acknowledgments

Among the many people who have helped with advice and encouragement, and over practical matters, in the preparation of this edition, I should particularly like to single out Peter Analytis and Paula de Chalus in London and Aliki Katselis in Athens, all three connected with the National Tourist Organisation of Greece. Thanks, too, are due to the Astir Hotel Company, which accommodated me in great style in Athens, and to my friend Christopher Kyd, who sacrificed some valuable holiday-time to drive me about the remoter reaches of Northern Greece.

The Author

Elisabeth de Stroumillo has been a travel journalist for over 25 years, both as a freelance and as Travel Correspondent and Travel Editor of The Daily Telegraph, London. Born in Paris and briefly resident there from time to time since, she has been on the move since her earliest childhood, living variously in India, Egypt, the United States and Europe. She has five other books to her credit: four volumes in her Tastes of Travel series, covering Normandy and Brittany, Western Loire and Aquitaine, North and Central Spain and Southern Spain, all including sections on regional gastronomy, plus a guide to Paris. Her awards include being chosen Britain's Travel Writer of the Year in 1986 and Ski Journalist of the Year (the Ski USA/Michelob Award) in 1987. She lives in London and is married to sculptor Philip Turner; they have two daughters.

Foreword

Travel in Greece has traditionally been more than just a matter of moving from one spot to another through a variety of land and sea-scapes. It has also involved journeying through time; a good part of civilised mankind's time upon this earth in fact. It has not merely meant exploring geographical and architectural features but also history and philosophy; at its best a spiritual experience as much as a visual one, and to do it full justice would require scholarship far greater than I can claim.

This book, therefore, does not attempt such a feat. Now in its third edition it is, rather, a distillation of some 25 years of travel in Greece that started, quite casually, with a succession of modest wanderings. Gradually I became addicted and, but for a few withdrawal-phases brought on by the grosser manifestations of mass tourism, my addiction has intensified ever since.

It is a truism to say that package tourism has to some extent blurred the more spiritually rewarding aspects of travel in Greece, but I do not believe that it has entirely destroyed them. Today's casual visitors, even the backpacking hedonists, are as likely as I was to become aware that there is more to the country than the immediate attractions of sun, sea and cheap wine. If this book helps them to discover even a small part of what Greece holds, it will have done its job. It is an attempt to create a bridge between the more superficial tourist office literature and the exhaustive, scholarly guide book.

It is hard to define Greece's unique magnetism. The quality of the light has something to do with it; there is a dawn-of-creation clarity about it in which, one feels, nothing sham can long survive. The austerity of the landscape is another factor; those awesome mountains that reflect every tint of the spectrum with the progress of the hours, and those bare islands piercing the surface of the restless sea. Although factories and power-stations are now commonplace; although tractors and other agricultural machines can be seen working everywhere in the plains, and engines now power most fishing-boats, Greek seas are still fished, inefficiently perhaps, by the traditional methods of centuries past and those careful terraces of vines and olives and fruit trees on the mountain foothills and in small valleys are still cultivated in much the same way as when they were first laboriously hand-hewn. One does not begrudge the Greeks their twentieth-century comforts, nor even the rewards of increasing tourism, yet one is grateful that there are still uncluttered, pristine landscapes, compounded solely of essential elements, if one wants to find them.

Foreword

And everywhere in this timeless landscape are, of course, visible legacies of the past: not just the famous ones like Olympia, Delphi, Knossos and the Parthenon but hundreds of lesser ones throughout the country, heightening the sensation of being in some curiously magic land where past and present co-exist. Broken columns rise from a cornfield; beneath an innocent-looking meadow is an Hellenic tomb; an out-of-the way village boasts an 11th century Byzantine chapel; even the little one-storeyed stone house on the hillside, surrounded by patches of corn, vegetables, a few vines and olives and a bevy of chickens, is a recognisable descendant of its most distant forebears.

The shepherd, stretched out in the shade of a tree as he watches his herd, wears his mass-produced trousers and shirt with the same fine carelessness as his ancestors wore their goatskins; the farmer hoeing a field that lies alongside a stretch of Mycaenean wall does so with a dignity that well becomes such a noble setting.

The village women, laughing and chattering as they do their washing at the edge of a river and then lay it to dry in the sun over clumps of thyme and oregano, are clearly Nausicaa's heiresses, and their treatment of the unexpected stranger arriving in their midst is in the same Homeric tradition. You can still turn up unheralded, even at the height of the tourist season, in almost any Greek town or village and a bed will be found for you, water will be produced for you to wash in and food will be set before you without expectation of any reward save the satisfaction of having observed the laws of hospitality. Mass-tourism hotels have eroded the tradition in places but the spirit behind it is not dead: the humblest *commis* waiter is at heart more a host than a servitor.

Politically, too, the Greeks are not so different from their ancestors. The cradle-of-democracy cliché is true enough, but it is only a part of the whole truth: throughout history, government in Greece has alternated between disorderly democracy and totalitarianism of one kind or another, and through it all the Greeks themselves have remained essentially the same: tough and resilient, sharply intelligent and inquisitive, essentially independent of spirit and, beyond a certain point, virtually ungovernable. Masters and men there may be, but it is not always easy to tell them apart: stripped to the waist aboard a luxury yacht the owner and his crew not only look indistinguishable but converse as equals, too.

The theories that govern the rendering of Greek words into English are varied in the extreme. I have tried to do it as phonetically as possible, to help readers not only with pronunciation but also to decipher road signs, on which the translations are apt to be phonetic renderings of the Greek. Since there is no "soft" C in Greek, I have therefore substituted K wherever practical. In many cases, however, there is a traditional form of English spelling and where this is misleading (Cyclades, Mycaenae) I have put the phonetic form in brackets alongside; where there is no ambiguity (Corinth, Corfu), I have left it unchanged. It should also be remembered that there is no special sound for the letter Y in modern Greek; both the y and i are pronounced as in "fit", or "feet", and not as in "why". Accents are used purely to indicate where stresses should be laid.

Population figures are approximate and indicated in brackets thus: (pop. c. xxxx).

General Information

How to get there

By Air

Olympic Airways, the national airline, operates between Athens and the capitals of Europe, the Middle East, Africa and the United States, most of its services reciprocated by the corresponding foreign national airlines. Other foreign airlines also link Athens with destinations not served by Olympic Airways. Olympic Airways and one or two other European airlines also connect the Northern Greek capital of Thessaloniki with points in Europe. Lowest high-season London-Athens scheduled return fare is currently just under £200 (advance-purchase excursion); lowest comparable New York-Athens is just under $1,000 return.

Athens Airport West (Olympic) and East (foreign airlines) terminals are a 30-minute coach ride from the Amalias Avenue city terminal (for East Terminal) and Aghios Kosmas/Othonos Street (for West Terminal). The fare is 160 drachmas including luggage. Taxis are plentiful and, from the airport to an hotel in the central area, should not cost more than 600 drachmas. An airport tax is levied on all departing passengers over 12 years old.

There are in addition scores of package-tour companies running their own charter flights to Greece from all over Europe, principally to carry holidaymakers on packaged inclusive deals. They do, however, sell seats on these charter flights to individual travellers for very much less than the cost of a seat on a scheduled service; the only drawbacks are that their flight-frequencies are more limited and that the authorities have become wary of "seat-onlys", thanks to the increasing number of feckless backpackers who use them. There is always the slight risk of an official clampdown that could compel the charter airline to fly such passengers straight home again.

The National Tourist Office of Greece maintains offices in most of the major capital cities of the world (in London at 197 Regent Street, W.1; in New York at Olympic Tower, 645 Fifth Avenue, New York 10022) which can supply the names of the principal inclusive holiday operators and a good deal of other information.

By Land and Sea
Rail services are run from most European capitals to Thessaloniki
and Athens; from London the journey is about 60 hours and costs
from about £135 return depending on the route (less for those under
26). The railways of Europe also run their own coach network
(Europabus) connecting most of the major cities with Thessaloniki,
Volos and Athens; from London the way is via Ostend, Munich and
Belgrade, the duration 3 days and the cost, including two overnight
stops with breakfast en route, around £125 return. Independent coach
operators also run various bus services, some with fewer overnight
stops (some with none) for considerably less.

From the Belgian Channel coast to the Greek border at Evzoni, it is
just under 2,880 kilometres (1,800 miles) by the fast route through
Belgium, Germany, Austria and Yugoslavia; four to six days' fairly
hard driving. An alternative for motorists is to put their cars on one
of the many ferries that ply from various Italian ports (notably Venice,
Ancona, Bari and Brindisi, either direct to Patras in the Peloponnese
or Piraeus, or via Corfu to Igoumenitsa on the western coast of Epirus,
Central Greece. Fares vary, obviously, with the size of car, length of
journey and number of passengers; as an example, a medium-sized
saloon with four adult passengers is about £150 ($265) one way from
Brindisi to Igoumenitsa by day, without meals or cabin accommodation.

Scheduled steamer services are operated to Patras in the Peloponnese
and/or Piraeus, the port of Athens, from several Western Mediterranean ports, including Dubrovnik and Split, Trieste and Venice, and
also from Limassol and Larnaca in Cyprus, Istanbul and Kusadasi in
Turkey, Alexandria in Egypt, the Black Sea port of Odessa, Lattakia in
Syria, and Haifa in Israel.

Travel within the Country
The cost of public transport, particularly on buses and ferries which
exist principally to serve the local population, is extremely reasonable
unless one goes first-class, with cabin accommodation, on ships.
Organised transport for tourists is more expensive but it often includes
meals and hotel accommodation. There are excellent conducted sightseeing tours by coach, and regular cruises in Greek waters lasting
for anything between one and fourteen days. It is also worth
remembering that day or half-day excursions to local sights are often
run by the local bus company as well as the coach-tour operators,
and at a much lower price.

Details of coach and cruise itineraries are to be found in the monthly
Greek Travel Pages guide, an invaluable aid sold in Athens from 12
Kimotikou Stakion Street, 176-71 Kallithea, and from travel agencies,
hotels, etc. In Britain it is also available from Timsway Holidays,

11

General Information

Nightingales Corner, Little Chalfont, Bucks HP7 9QS.

Buses
The bus system, particularly on longer-distance routes, is operated with modern, comfortable vehicles that run frequently and surprisingly punctually, although working out and pricing itineraries involving several stops can take time and tax patience. There are terminals in all the main towns (two in Athens) and each area of the country is served by a differently numbered network; careful enquiries should be made as to which network (each has a different booking office) to take. Local buses tend to serve local needs (market days, etc.) and are less sophisticated. The *Greek Travel Pages* guide provides the necessary information.

Rail
There are only two main railway lines: from Athens northwards to Thessaloniki and the Yugoslav border, and southwards to Kalamata in the Peloponnese. The Athens railway stations are next to each other in Theodorou Deligianni, north-west of Ommonia Square. Larissas Station serves the northern line and Peloponissou the southern.

Ferries
Most inter-island ferries operate out of Piraeus, but there is an increasing number of scheduled local services running from Thessaloniki, Kavala, Volos, Aghios Konstantinos and Kymi (to the Sporades), Rafina and Lavrion (to the Cyclades), Patras and Kyllini (to the Ionians), and Gytheion (to Crete). Travellers with limited time who want to visit several islands need to study these routes carefully. They may make it possible to island-hop in a more random fashion than previously, when it was almost essential to confine oneself to islands on the same ferry-route, or to return between each one to Piraeus. There are also car ferries across the Gulf of Corinth. Here again, the *Greek Travel Pages* is essential since many travel agencies act only for certain steamship lines.

Taxis
Metered taxis, plentiful in most towns of any size, are hired from ranks. Non-metered taxis, available in most villages and distinguished by the sign ΑΓΟΡΑΙΟ, should be priced beforehand and a fare agreed for the trip.

Car Hire and Driving
The international firms like Avis and Hertz maintain offices in both Athens and Thessaloniki (see below) and operate through agents elsewhere; there are also numerous local firms. Prices vary with the season and the type of car but are not cheap since cars in Greece are heavily taxed. As a guide, a small car from a major international rental firm, with unlimited mileage, will cost about £185 ($315) per

week in the low season, including full insurance.

Cars will be delivered to the nearest airport free of charge and hire requirements are that drivers should be over 21 and in possession of a valid British, American or International Driving Licence.

Private cars may come into Greece with minimal frontier formalities for up to one year. Third-party insurance is compulsory: either a valid Green Card (from Britain) or short-term cover purchased at the border. The Automobile and Touring Club of Greece (ELPA) offers reciprocal assistance services to card-carrying members of other national motoring organisations.

The rule of the road is to keep to the right, but main road traffic has priority over that from side roads. (On side roads themselves, although many have been immeasurably improved in recent years, anything may happen and vigilance is the best rule.) Two roads are of international highway (if not motorway) standard: from the Yugoslav frontier to Thessaloniki and Athens, and from Athens to Corinth and westwards along the northern coast of the Peloponnese to Patras. Other roads vary from the new, fairly new, and very good though often narrow, down to hard-packed, unsurfaced but passable tracks — some of which lead to very desirable destinations — but as traffic in the country, particularly out of season, is on the light side, problems are few. Michelin Map No 980 is excellent.

In the major cities, particularly Athens and Thessaloniki, traffic is heavy, parking difficult, and many of the streets one-way. Petrol is sold by the litre and stations are adequately spaced on main roads; the cost of supergrade (not always available in small places) is around 80 drachmas a litre. There are also regulations limiting driving (particularly in Athens in an attempt to reduce pollution), though foreigners driving their own or hired cars are unlikely to be prosecuted.

The main car-hire companies:
Avis: 48 Amalias Avenue, Athens (tel. 322-4951); 71 Akti Miaouli, Piraeus (tel. 452-0639); 3 Nikis Avenue, Thessaloniki (tel. 031-227126); 3 Alexandras Avenue, Corfu (tel. 0661-38820); 25th August Street, Iraklion, Crete (tel. 081-225421); 9 Gallias Street, Rhodes (tel. 0241-24990).
Hertz: 12 Syngrou Avenue, Athens (tel. 922-0102); 9-11 Ag. Nikolaou Street, Piraeus (tel. 452-6600); 4 Venizelou Street, Thessaloniki (tel. 031-224906); 44 25th August Avenue, Iraklion, Crete (tel. 081-229702); 10 Grivas Street, Rhodes (tel. 0241-21819); also at six other locations.
Hellascars: 7 Stadiou Street, Athens (tel. 923-5353); 8 Venizelou Street, Thessaloniki (tel. 031-223927).
Budget and Interent are two other sizeable car-rental firms.

The Automobile & Touring Club of Greece has its head office at 2

General Information

Messoghion Street, Athens; there are branches in Agrinion, Corfu, Iraklion, Ioannina, Kalamata, Kavala, Khania, Lamia, Larissa, Patras, Thessaloniki and Volos, and at frontier posts.

Moped and Scooter Hire

Mopeds and scooters are available for hire in all popular resorts, but hirers should be aware of their drawbacks. They have probably been ridden hard by other tourists for two or more seasons and are thus hardly in prime condition; they are almost certainly inadequately insured (so carry your own accident cover), and crash helmets, though mandatory under Greek law, are not always provided.

Yacht Hire

Yacht hire is becoming increasingly popular; among the best-established firms, with offices both in London and Piraeus, are Camper & Nicholson (16 Regency Street, London SW1) and Halsey Marine International (22 Boston Place, London NW1).

There are three yacht associations: The Greek Yachtbrokers and Consultants Association, the Greek Bareboat Yacht Association, and the Hellenic Professional Yacht Owners Association, plus over 50 yacht brokers; for addresses, contact the nearest office of the National Tourist Organisation of Greece. Several specialist UK organisations also offer sailing package holidays.

Accommodation

Hotels

Hotels are officially classified as de luxe, A, B, C (Γ), D and E, though there are plans to change to a 'star' grading system in the not-too-distant future. It is by no means necessary to choose de luxe or A-class hotels to be comfortable; many Γ-class and D-class hotels have a high proportion of private baths and compensate in friendliness and cleanliness for what they may lack in luxury frills. Additionally, thousands of private houses have rooms to let and are also vetted. The 'Xenia' hotels, originally built and run by the National Tourist Organisation to provide accommodation in out-of-the-way places, have now in some cases been sold or leased to private hoteliers; 26 are still owned by the National Tourist Organisation and are listed in a special leaflet.

Traditional Settlements

Another National Tourist Organisation initiative has been to acquire a number of old and often part-derelict properties that were built in the traditional styles of their particular areas and renovate them for letting to tourists. There is now such accommodation for rent in seven settlements: Areopolis in the Mani, Oia on Thera (Santorini), Makrinitsa and Vizitsa in Pelion, Mesta on Chios, Papingo in Epiros, and the island of Psara, off Chios. Rentals can be arranged through the

National Tourist Organisation.

Camping and youth-hostelling
Well-laid out and equipped camp-sites, many of them run by the
National Tourist Organisation or by the Automobile and Touring Club
(ELPA) are to be found all over the country, at major inland tourist
honeypots (Olympia, Meteora, etc.) as well as by the sea. It is illegal
to camp elsewhere and, thanks to the depredations of selfish *al fresco*
campers, both private landowners and the authorities are not often
inclined to take a lenient view of those who do.

Members of overseas Youth Hostel Associations may use Greek
hostels, of which there are four in Athens and others in Delphi, Lito-
choro on Mount Olympos, Mycaenae, Nafplion, Olympia, Patras and
Thessaloniki. The Greek Youth Hostels Association is at 4 Dragatsaniou
Street, Athens; the YWCA is at 11 Amerikis Street, Athens, and the
YMCA at 28 Omirou Street, Athens.

Church Services
Over 85 per cent of the population is of the Greek Orthodox faith
and, outside of Athens which has both English and American (Pro-
testant) churches and a Roman Catholic church, there are few non-
Orthodox churches to be found.

Climate
From May to the end of October unbroken sunshine is the rule rather
than the exception in most of Greece: if the sky should cloud over or
a shower should fall, it is a rare occurrence except at the start and
end of the season, and visitors can console themselves with the
thought that rain is welcome on the parched land. On the other hand,
there is nearly always a light breeze to mitigate the extreme heat
and, in the Aegean area in July and August, this becomes the *meltemi*
wind which can make seas very rough. Most of the rainfall takes
place between November and February and in short, heavy bursts
that are interspersed with long, bright and often warm periods. Snow
is rare except on the highest peaks of the Pindos, Taygetos, Olympos,
Parnassos, Pelion and Cretan White Mountain ranges, on some of
which winter-sports facilities are being built. When it falls in Athens,
it seldom lies for more than a few hours so, for serious touring and
sightseeing, winter is almost the best season, when crowds are sparse.
February, March and April, though the sea is still chilly, bring myriads
of brilliant flowers and a profusion of tender vegetables; September
and October, though the land by then is dry and sere, is perfect for
those who enjoy warm seas to swim in.

Currency, Credit Cards and Banking
The Greek currency unit is the drachma, subdivided into 100 lepta.

General Information

Coins are to the value of 2, 5, 10, 20 and 50 lepta; 1, 2, 4, 10, 20 and 50 drachmas. Notes are for 50, 100, 500 and 1,000 drachmas, although the 50-drachma note is becoming rarer as the new coins come into circulation. All banks, travel bureaux, classified hotels and some tourist shops will change money or travellers cheques, and at the prevailing bank rate; only a handful of the more sophisticated Athens restaurants will do so. Banking hours, except on Saturdays, Sundays and holidays, are 0800 to 1400. In larger cities, there is limited afternoon opening for bureaux-de-change.

Eurocheques are accepted at banks everywhere and at many shops; major credit cards are becoming more widely accepted at restaurants, shops and occasionally petrol stations.

Customs and Immigration

Every traveller may bring in up to 25,000 drachmas in Greek money and an unlimited amount of foreign currency and used personal possessions including a transistor radio, up to two cameras — though you should declare the second camera and ask the Customs officer to write down the details in your passport — binoculars, etc. Two hunded cigarettes per person are also permitted (foreign ones, only on sale in a few major cities and luxury international hotels, are extremely expensive) and one bottle of spirits. Virtually any amount of souvenir purchases can be taken out of Greece but there is a strict ban on the export of all antiquities unless they are accompanied by a certificate from the Archaeological Service, 13 Polygnotou Street, Athens.

A valid passport, though not a visa, is required of all British, Commonwealth and United States nationals staying for up to three months. There are no health requirements for persons arriving directly from Britain or the United States and Canada. Certain other immunisations may be necessary for those arriving from parts of Africa, the Orient and beyond; check before departure.

Dress and Cosmetics

Even at the height of summer, particularly in the Islands, it can be cool and breezy in the evenings, so a cardigan or some sort of warm wrap is essential. In winter a topcoat and a light raincoat or umbrella are necessary, as well as versatile clothing that can be adapted to changes in temperature. In the major cities, however many tourist sights they may contain, extremely casual dress is regarded somewhat askance, and in many monasteries and churches it is forbidden entirely; in the resorts, the opposite is the case: bikinis and the most minimal shorts cause no offence. Nudity and toplessness on public beaches, unfortunately on the increase, is liable to shock — and arouse overt hostility.

Cosmetics and the blander international varieties of patent medicines
are available in most of the sizeable towns and resorts but are taxed
as luxuries and therefore cost more than they would at home.

Hairdressing
Although a visit to the barber is part of every male Greek's routine
and barbers' shops are everywhere, women's hairdressers are usually
only found in the bigger towns and resorts and, of course, in the
more expensive hotels.

Embassies and Consulates
Australia: 37D Soutsou Street, 115-21 Athens.
Canada: 4 Ghennadiou Street, 115-21 Athens.
U K: 1 Ploutarchou, 106-75 Athens; 8 Venizelou Street, Eleftherias
Square, Thessaloniki; also Vice-Consulates in Corfu, Iraklion (Crete),
Kavala, Patras, Rhodes and Samos.
U S A: 91 Vassilis Sophias Avenue, 115-21 Athens.

Etiquette
Tourists, from Pausanias onwards, have long been a familiar sight to
the Greeks and their strange ways arouse some curiosity but little
condemnation except in holy places. On the other hand, as has not
infrequently been pointed out, the word *"xenos"* stands both for
"stranger" and "guest" and it is as important not to offend the Greek
tradition of hospitality as it is not to abuse it. A cup of coffee or a
drink and ten minutes conversation is often a far more appropriate
return than a tip for a kindly service. In some circumstances where a
tip does seem appropriate, it will be better received if it is offered
"for the children" (see below).

Among themselves, Greeks observe certain formalities and codes
which need not affect the foreigner so long as he recognises their
existence. Although Greek women are far more "liberated" than they
were even a decade ago, unmarried country girls are carefully protected and sheltered and in more rural areas still get dowries; neither
they nor married women often serve in restaurants, nor do wives
usually accompany their husbands to the cafés (*kaffeneions*). Unless
close friends, Greeks address each other formally: Nikolaos Kotsis,
for example, is Kyrie Kotsis or, when slightly better acquainted, Kyrie
Niko.

Curiosity is an integral part of the Greek character and it is not rude
to ask seemingly personal questions ("Have you children?" "What's
your job?" and so on) but when one knows the Greeks better one
realises that they draw a firm line between natural curiosity and prying,
and know when to respect privacy. The same applies in reverse, of
course: one must not presume too much upon their friendship nor

seek to probe sensitive subjects; they are, for instance, often remarkably well-informed on world affairs and happy to discuss them probingly and at length, but less objective concerning matters nearer their hearts, such as Cyprus and Turkey.

The foreigner who studies their social conventions and abides by them will get to know them best: when invited to a Greek home it is essential to partake of the formal refreshment offered and polite to bring flowers or an edible gift such as chocolates. A similar offering is traditional on "name days" (the day of the saint after whom the person is named) which are celebrated more than birthdays; and a present to or for the children of a family is more acceptable as a return courtesy than a tip or a present for the adults, for children are beloved to the point of adulation.

Festivals and Entertainment

The theatre is still very much alive in Athens, (including outdoor performances of ballet, opera, concerts and classical dramas in Athens during the summer Festival period), *Son et Lumière* on the Acropolis from April to October (English language version 2000 hrs). Theatre and music festivals and *Son et Lumière* performances are also held in various other places, such as Epidauros in the Peloponnese, Dodona in Epirus, Rhodes, Corfu, Thessaloniki and Philippi in Macedonia, Thassos, etc. There are also summer Wine Festivals, tasting unlimited, entrance about 250 drs, at Daphni just outside Athens, at Alexandroupolis, in Rhodes and Crete.

Otherwise there is the cinema and, increasingly, home videos, in which there has been a notable boom in recent years, to the threatened detriment of what was traditionally the favourite occupation of all: café-chat. However, it will take many generations of changing habits to outmode completely the *volta,* or evening stroll, when people turn out in their best to swap gossip and enjoy the cool air and pause for modest refreshment at the outdoor tables of the local *kaffeneions.* There are *bouzouki* places and nightclubs in Athens, its suburbs and Thessaloniki (even casinos on Mount Parnes, Athens, in the Achilleon, Corfu, in Sithonia and on Rhodes) and discothèques in many tourist resorts, large and small, but the Greek himself is not, by and large, a nightclub addict. When he feels like dancing or singing, it is more likely to be a spontaneous affair in the *kaffeneion* or *taverna* with one of the customers providing the music.

Apart from Carnival (a three-week period ending on the Monday before Lent), at its most exuberant in the Plaka quarter of Athens and in Patras, but celebrated cheerfully everywhere, the most important Greek festival is Easter (especially the Sunday, when the Paschal lamb is roasted in the main square and everybody sings or dances after the feast). Christmas is a more subdued occasion; Epiphany is marked by the ceremony of the Blessing of the Waters.

Food and Drink

It was the Grecophile author Robert Liddell who observed that the measure of one's love for Greece was one's willingness to put up with its cuisine and there is no point pretending that Greek cooking will satisfy the gourmet. Nor is it improved in most package-tour hotels by concessions to so-called international tastes. On the other hand, if one knows what to look for, the fare in the simpler *tavernas* or restaurants can be very adequate and often good. Meat is not allowed to hang properly and is haphazardly cut, so except at a *psistaria* (grill-restaurant) and expensive big-city restaurants, steaks and grills should be avoided. However, small pieces on skewers (*souvláki*, pronounced souv-lie-kee), young spit-roasted lamb or sucking pig in early spring, and stews (*stiphádo*) are all good. Fish nowadays, thanks to increased demand and over-fishing, is often frozen, but vegetables and fruit are all fresh and delicious; olive oil is of excellent quality.

The practice of "having a look in the kitchen" before ordering a meal is not merely a convenient way of overcoming the language barrier; Greeks themselves do it because it allows them to judge the quality of what is on offer. A dish called by a local or unfamiliar name often proves irresistible when actually inspected on the stove.

Various dishes
Dishes ordered together tend all to arrive on the table together, for Greeks like to pick at different dishes (including each others') simultaneously, and do not insist on food being piping hot. Those who like their starters before their main course should have them with their apéritifs, and order the main course later. Among the best known starters, or *mezedes*, are *taramosaláta*, smoked fish-roe paté; *melitzánosalata*, aubergine paté with lots of garlic; *tsatsiki*, thick yoghurt with cucumber and garlic; *spanakópitta* or *tirópitta*, flaky spinach-and-cheese or cheese-only pies; *oktopódhi* or *kalamarákia*, small pieces of octopus or squid. *Psarósoupa* is a fish soup that is almost a meal in itself; *barboúnia* (red mullet), *lithrina* (bass) and *synagridha* (bream), all grilled, are excellent popular fish. Main meat courses worth trying are *fricassé*, lamb stewed with green vegetables and egg-and-lemon sauce; *keftédes*, spiced meatballs; *dolmádes*, stuffed vine leaves; and *moussaká*, minced meat, potato, aubergine, courgette and onion in layers, topped by crisp-baked béchamel sauce; *yiouvétsi* (lamb with spaghetti). *Skordhaliá*, a purée of potato with olive oil, garlic and lemon juice, is the Greek equivalent of *aioli* and delicious with fried fish. Anything *yemistá* (stuffed), be it tomatoes, aubergines, courgettes or sweet peppers, is generally good, though the stuffing is more likely to be of rice and herbs than meat, and there are nearly always pastas and fried potato chips available.

19

General Information

Desserts are almost invariably fruit, or one can have white mild *fetta* goat cheese.

Eating places

An eating place is called an *estiatório* (restaurant) or *taverna* (tavern) or *psistaria* (literally, "roastery" — specialising in grills); they invariably serve wine but not always apéritifs. A *kaffeneion* (café) on the other hand serves ouzo, the aniseed-flavoured spirituous national drink, and other hard liquors as well as coffee, but rarely wine. A *zaharoplastéion* (pastry shop) will also have coffee and spirits, but specialises in yoghurt, baked custards, ice creams and traditional confections. Travellers staying in privately rented rooms rather than hotels can find the equivalent of breakfast (bread, butter, honey and coffee) at a *galaktopoleion*: literally, a dairy.

Instant coffee, espresso and cappucino are increasingly available throughout Greece and, in some sophsticated cafés, you may be told that Greek coffee is not available, though by law it should be, and is therefore often made nowadays with the modern heating-element rather than over flame. The result is far less satisfactory than traditional Greek coffee, which comes in three varieties: *glykó* (sweet), *métreo* (medium-sweet) and *skéto* (without sugar).

Wine

The staple table wine of Greece is *retsina,* a light, resin-flavoured white wine that varies in quality from place to place (and often from restaurant to restaurant if the owner has his own vineyard; those who do not take to it should ask for *krasi áretsinato* (unresinated wine). *Retsina* often comes straight from a barrel (*khéma,* or "loose"); unresinated wine is more often bottled. Labels to look for include Boutari's Lac des Roches, Kambas Hymettos, Santa Helena, and Nemea (which also produces a good rosé). More expensive and also closer to the equivalent French wines are the Porto Carras brands. Water is safe to drink almost everywhere.

Gratuities and Bargaining

Tips are recognised for certain services, detailed below, but for many freely-given services they can easily offend, as explained under "Etiquette". However, porters at railway stations, air terminals, hotels etc. should get about 25 drachmas per piece of baggage carried; taxi drivers 10 to 15 per cent of the fare; hairdressers, cloakroom and hotel staff similar to what they would receive for those services in England. In restaurants, the bill normally includes a percentage for service, which can be rounded out and the result left on the plate to show particular appreciation to the waiter himself. In addition, between 50 and 100 drachmas (according to the size of the bill) should also be left on the table for, or given to, the youngster or commis waiter (*micrós* pronounced mee-kross) who has cleared the plates, etc. In places where service is not included, leave between 12 per cent and 20 per cent of the bill, depending on the degree of luxury involved. Bargaining is not indispensable to shopping in Greece except perhaps in the Athens flea market, though many shopkeepers will "round down" the total if the amount warrants it, and a Greek may consider one foolish if one doesn't at least request a better price.

Language

This is less of a problem than one might at first suppose. So many Greeks have emigrated — to America, Australia, Africa and elsewhere — to make their fortunes, and then returned home to enjoy them, that there is scarcely a village, however remote, that does not contain someone with some command of English. The best way to locate him, if one needs an interpreter, is to sit at the main *kaffeneion* (café), hopefully ask the waiter if he speaks English (meelá-tay angleeká?), and the linguist will eventually be produced. In restaurants, even fairly chic ones, it is common practice to visit the kitchen and point to what one wants to eat, recommended even if it is not necessary to obviate the problem of deciphering menus (see under Food and Drink). However, a phrase book is undoubtedly an asset, not least because it should include the Greek alphabet which is indispensable, especially to motorists, for reading signs. Most directional signs and town names are printed in Roman as well as Greek characters, but many an interesting sight can be missed if one is unable to recognise the words *APXAIOΛOΓIKO XOPIO* or *APXAIEO XOPIO* (archaeological or ancient site or place) which is often the only indication of the less touristically popular sites. In cases of difficulty, most sizeable towns and seaside resorts have, if not a tourist information office, tourist policemen (distinguished by white shoulder badges) who understand at least one foreign language and, of course, staff in the more luxurious hotels are perfectly fluent in English.

Lavatories

In hotels, right down the scale to D and even E class, few nasty surprises await the visitor. Elsewhere — in modest pensions, private houses, all but the grandest restaurants and all but the most palatial filling stations — Greek plumbing is still rooted in the not-so-distant days when the lavatory-roll was an undreamed-of luxury for the vast majority of people. Instead, they used carefully torn-up sheets of old newspaper, suspended from a rough wire hoop attached to the wall, or from a long, stout nail. Many of us learned the rudiments of reading in Greek from these piecemeal scraps, in fact, and felt almost cheated when a story abruptly stopped just as we were getting on nicely with it. Flushing them away, however, was beyond the capacity of the average domestic plumbing system and they had to be deposited, when no longer legible, in a waste-paper bin from which they were eventually taken for burning. Today although plumbing is more efficient and paper more readily disposable, the waste-paper bin habit survives at less sophisticated social levels, and we old hands not only respect it but also experience a certain nostalgia when we meet one.

In the realms of the public convenience, most sizeable towns are these days furnished with at least one, and some are as modern as anyone could possibly wish them to be: the one in Athens' Kolonaki Square being, literally, a shining example. Unfortunately, though, many are semi-permanently closed, not because their standards of hygiene are in any way deficient, but because the problem of staffing them appears to be insurmountable.

Photography

In the main centres black and white film can only occasionally be found, but colour film is readily available (though more expensive than in England or the United States) either at photographers' shops or tourist shops. The former can process both black and white and colour prints, but transparencies must be made in Athens. In taking photographs, remember that the light in Greece is extraordinarily clear: an ultra violet filter is a great asset, and the best pictures are taken in the mornings before the sun is too high or after 1600 hours.

Postal Information

Mail does not automatically go by air unless so marked (AEPOII-OPIKO<u>Σ</u>). Airmail postcards to Britain and most other European countries and letters weighing less than 20 grammes cost 40 drachmas (Europe) and 50 drachmas (other countries); letters weighing from 20 up to 50 grammes cost 90 drachmas (Europe) and 110 drachmas (other countries). Internal mail tends to be slow but telegrams are reasonably cheap and quick and the telephone system has largely been converted to subscriber trunk dialling and is fairly efficient, although smaller villages and islands may be short of public telephone kiosks.

Stamps can be bought and telegrams sometimes sent from the post office (*TAXY△POMEION*); the telephone offices (O.T.E.) are separate and telegrams are normally sent from them. Additionally, the ubiquitous *periptero* or street kiosk, open up to 24 hours a day in big cities, often has a public telephone and also sells stamps as well as a host of other useful things like toothpaste, shaving cream, writing paper, sweets, cigarettes and newspapers. Letters sent *Poste Restante* will go to the main post office; the word "Esq" should be left out.

Public Holidays

New Year's Day; January 6 (Epiphany); "Clean Monday" (the Monday before Lent); March 25 (Independence Day); the Orthodox Good Friday, Easter Day and Easter Monday; May 1; August 15 (Assumption); October 28 ("Ohi" or National Day); Christmas Day and December 26 (St Stephen). Carnival, which lasts for the three weeks (particularly at weekends) before Clean Monday, reaches its peak on the final Sunday and is celebrated in towns and villages alike. Easter is the most important religious festival and Lent is observed seriously.

Shopping Hours

There has been much experimentation with shopping hours, particularly in Athens and hard-and-fast rules are yet to be established. At the time of writing (July 1988) shops were open 0800-1400 and 1730-2030 on Tuesdays, Thursdays and Fridays; 0800-1500 on Wednesdays and Saturdays; 1330-2030 on Mondays. However in areas where there is self-catering accommodation for tourists, food shops stay open far longer (and open on Sunday mornings, too); and souvenir shops rarely close either.

Sightseeing

Museums, archaeological sites and other important sites are almost all closed on Tuesdays (but, confusingly, sometimes on Mondays instead). From April 1 until October 31, the official summer season, major museums and sites are open from 0800 until 1730 or 1800 (in the text, this is indicated as "all day"); less popular museums and sites from about 0845 or 0900 until 1500 (indicated in the text as "until mid-afternoon"). In the winter season, and on Sundays and holidays, opening hours are often shorter and should be checked locally. On the following major holidays, most sites and museums remain closed all day: January 1, March 25, the Friday and Sunday of the Orthodox Easter, and Christmas Day.

Entrance charges at the time of writing varied from 100 drachmas to 600 drachmas, but as they are liable to frequent change they are not given in the text. Holders of student cards pay reduced fees, but there are no longer free-admission days at most sites.

Sports

The simplest water sports predominate: swimming, snorkelling, underwater fishing, etc., though board-sailing, paragliding and water-skiing are increasingly available in better-developed places. Sailing and yachting facilities are expanding (see under 'Travel within the Country' above). There are local sailing clubs at Vouliagmeni and Phaleron Bay, near Athens, and in Corfu, Volos and Thessaloniki among other places.

On land, too (perhaps because walking is still the most usual form of

23

General Information

locomotion), sport is mostly of the less sophisticated variety. There are only four golf courses in the country: an old-established one near Athens; one on Rhodes; one on Corfu, and another in shipowner John Carras's new resort of Porto Carras in Sithonia, northern Greece. Public tennis courts, as distinct from hotel ones, are few and far between, though the Tourist Organisation has installed them at some of its public swimming beaches and camping grounds, and there are tennis clubs in Athens, Thessaloniki, Corfu, Crete and Rhodes.

Mountaineering is fairly well catered for, and skiing is becoming more ubiquitous on the winter scene. Parnassos, Olympos and Florina are the best developed areas: information from the Greek Skiing and Alpine Federation, 7 Karageorgi Servias Street, Athens.

Athletic displays are held in the modern stadium in Athens, and there is a racecourse at Phaleron, just outside the city. Cricket of a sort is played on Corfu; amateur football is popular and taken seriously everywhere, but there are few organised spectator sports.

Tourist Offices

The National Tourist Organisation of Greece has information offices at:
Athens: 2 Karageorgi Servias Street (inside the National Bank of Greece building), 4 Stadiou Street (Spyromiliou Arcade), and Hellenikon Airport East
Corfu: Dhikitiriou Building
Crete: 6 Akti Tobasi, Khania; 1 Xanthoulidou Street, Iraklion
Ioannina: 2 Zerva Street
Larissa: 18 Koumoundourou Street
Patras: Neos Methorikas Stathmos, Glyfada
Rhodes: Makarios and Papagou Streets
Thessaloniki: 8 Aristotelous Square
Volos: Riga Ferraiou Square

The Country
and its History

The Country

Over 60 per cent of Greece is mountainous. Widespread neglect and deforestation during the years of Turkish occupation, and Greece's subsequent impoverishment, also left much of it barren except for gorse, scrub, coarse grass and thorn bushes. Today, however, newly replanted mountainsides and acres of maturing forests are becoming almost commonplace sights on the mainland, particularly in the north-west. Most of the large cultivable plains are in the centre and north of the mainland — Macedonia and Epirus principally; elsewhere cultivation is limited to small plains and valleys and the foothills around them. Rivers are few, and most of them tend to dry up in summer; this lack of water despite new irrigation projects, combined with topographical hindrances, makes hard work of agriculture.

The Greek coastline, not counting the islands, is 9,000 miles long and much of it, like the landscape, is precipitous and rocky. Beaches exist in plenty but, since their popularity is a comparatively modern phenomenon, many of them can only be reached by boat: the sites of seaside towns were originally chosen for their suitability as harbours rather than bathing resorts. The harshness of the Greek land- and seascapes, however, gives them a dramatic quality un-equalled anywhere: a piercing, uncluttered beauty of line that, com-bined with the purity of the ever-changing light, is quite unforgettable. In this often stark setting, trees are doubly lovely: the sudden luxuriance of a group of ancient planes around a spring, of an oak or chestnut forest on the slopes of Pelion, of newly-afforested slopes bravely bristling with infant conifers or deciduous trees, of the greenery of such northerly islands as Corfu, Skiathos and Thassos. And everywhere the dark exclamation marks of cypress trees and poplars, together with the more recently introduced eucalyptus, give depth and contrast to the more barren scene.

Flora and Fauna

From July onwards, when most tourists visit Greece, the countryside is parched and yellow-brown, with only the brilliant colours of oleander, bougainvillea, geranium, other heat-loving flowers and a few brave roses to relieve it. Where there is water, there are also green trees; otherwise the only verdance is the silvery-sheening olives and the dark cypresses to alternate with the sere tawnyness of the fields, the greys and violets of the herb-covered hills and the blues of sea and sky.

In winter and spring, however, Greece becomes a different place: with the first rains, tender shoots of grass spring magically out of the dry ground, the dusty leaves of orange and lemon trees take on a dark gloss and the fruit begins to ripen on their branches. Emerald-coloured winter corn softens the fields, myriads of wild flowers and shrubs burst into bloom — poppies, asphodel, euphorbia, freesias, narcissi, croci, wild orchids and hyacinths, daisies, judas and acacia trees. By February the countryside is a riot of colour with mimosa, cherry, apricot and almond blossom burgeoning in turn. Every type of fruit and vegetable grows and thanks to modern market-gardening techniques, for longer seasons than in the past: lettuces, cabbages, beans, peas, artichokes carrots, spinach, okra, dill and all the other aromatic herbs; strawberries, mulberries, cherries, peaches, plums, apricots, tangerines, bananas, oranges and apples.

By the time most of these are over, in June, the melons, figs, grapes, pomegranates, tomatoes, aubergines and courgettes have already taken over. Olive trees are everywhere and so are carobs; planes are the principal shade-trees.

Wildlife is sparse: there are few snakes, though plenty of lizards and miscellaneous insects (including flies, of course, and some tiresome midges and mosquitoes in marshy spots), and some wild boar, wolves, bears, foxes, rabbits and hares. Common birds, as well as the seagull, include wild duck, hawks, eagles, pheasant and woodcock, partridge and quail. The domestic beast of burden is the donkey though horses and mules are also used, particularly in the north. Goats are prolific, even more so than sheep; cows are mostly found on the plains of the north; pigs and chickens are also kept in great numbers. All the better-known Mediterranean fish are found in Greek waters (though over-fishing has reduced their numbers and pushed up prices), ranging from the swordfish down through bass, bream and mullet to white-bait; crayfish, octopus and squid are also available, though the crustaceans are becoming more scarce and are even imported.

History

Men have inhabited Greece from earliest times: since Homo Sapiens himself, in fact; there are many traces of Stone Age man in the central and northern parts of the country, dating back to the 7th millennium BC. Best known, however, are the remains of the Early Bronze Age (3rd millennium BC) and subsequent periods, when Greece began to come under the influence of lands to the east of the Mediterranean, and of the Egyptians.

The early Helladic sites on the mainland and in the Peloponnese, and the early Minoan sites of eastern Crete are relics of these ages; also the early Cycladic (Kikladic) culture, for the islands were important stepping stones between the two. After 2000 BC, invaders, possibly the first actual Greeks, made inroads into the mainland and broke the cultural continuity there, but at first left the Minoans on Crete alone.

Minoans, Mycaeneans and Dorians

The Minoans, it was until recently believed, were a wholly peaceable people, engrossed in building and embellishing their great palaces, engaging in ritualistic sports like bull-leaping, refining their arts and appearance (particularly the elaborately-coiffed, topless ladies) extending their trade — and thereby quietly colonising nearby Aegean islands — until the aftermath of the catastrophic eruption of Thera (Santorini) virtually wiped out their civilisation in about 1450 BC.

Recent excavations, however, suggest that the Minoans were altogether more barbarous and brutal, and weakened their own civilisation through civil wars well before the Santorini earthquake. It also now seems likely that Crete had been invaded by the warlike Mycaeneans (Mikineans), who by this time had emerged as an ethnic and cultural entity on the mainland. If these new theories continue to gain scientific support, then human elements contributed as much to the destruction of the Minoan power-centres as did natural calamities. That there had been communication between the two civilisations has long been recognised, even in legend: Theseus, after all, was rescuing Athens from its punitive obligations to King Minos of Crete, after whom modern archaeologists called the entire Cretan civilisation.

The Mycaeneans, with their massively fortified palace-cities, were in any case a far more warlike people, their best-known and longest-lasting confict being, of course, the Trojan War, but even they fell before the next waves of invaders, the Dorians from the North. Only Athens escaped the onslaught of these barbarians and thus laid the foundations for her future pre-eminence in Greek history. Refugees from other former strongholds, now devastated, found their way there, as they did eventually to various points on the Aegean shores of Asia Minor. The unity of the Mycaenean, or Late Bronze Age, civilisation had been shattered and a so-called Dark Age (11th-8th centuries BC) followed, during which scattered settlements, separated by the mountains and the seas, turned inward upon themselves.

City States

From these settlements were gradually born the self-governing Hellenic city-states which were to be the bases of Greek political, social and economic life for the next 800 years encompassing, in terms of art, three major periods: the Archaic (700-500 BC), Classical (500-300 BC) and Hellenistic (300-100 BC).

The Country and its History

Most of these city-states of which Athens, including most of Attica, was the largest, had certain things in common: strong defences against the depredations of their rivals; an acropolis where the temples and other places of worship were concentrated; an *agora*, or central market-cum-meeting-place; a theatre, and a stadium or gymnasium. All these public buildings were impressive; houses remained modest until a much later age. Outside the city-states and their immediate territory of arable land, shrines and sanctuaries (such as those of Apollo at Delphi and Delos, of Zeus at Olympia and Dodona, and many lesser ones) were the only civilised centres. Here the more belligerent rivalries were sublimated in athletic contests and in out-doing one another in the splendour of architectural and artistic offerings to the presiding deity.

The rivalry between the city-states was partially suspended during the early 5th century BC when a threat arose from Persia, overseas. For just over 20 years, until Xerxes was finally routed both at sea (Salamis, 480 BC, and Mykali, near Samos, 479 BC) and on land (Marathon, 490 BC), Athens and to a lesser extent Sparta led all Greece against the foe. Thereafter began the so-called Golden Age of the 5th and 4th centuries BC, during which Athenian culture achieved its zenith.

But eventually even Athens fell to Sparta and her allies in 404 BC, ending the crippling Peloponnesian War, and perpetual strife between the city-states became the rule until most of them fell to Macedon, the new power from the north, led first by Philip and then by his son Alexander the Great until the latter's death in 323 BC.

Romans
The independence of Greece then came to its close with the Pax Romana and the incorporation of much of the country into the Roman Empire in 27 BC. Rome had, however, been absorbing Greek culture for long before this, both from the mainland and its colonies of Magna Graecia (now Sicily and Southern Italy), and she repaid her debt by keeping the country peaceful for the next 300 years.

Corinth, and not Athens (though it was important intellectually), was the centre of Roman rule in the Greek province of Achaea until Rome in its turn began to lose power to the new Christian capital of Byzantium, or Constantinople, founded in 330 AD by the Emperor Constantine.

Byzantium and the Ottomans
Then Greece became a Byzantine stronghold and Salonika (now Thessaloniki) its most important city. The country was still relatively protected, but the city-states dwindled in strength and many became prey to invaders. When Constantinople itself was sacked and weakened by the members of the iniquitous 4th Crusade in 1204, the

Greek mainland was an easier target for conquest than the Holy Land. Feudal Franks carved themselves domains from Athens herself and throughout the Peloponnese; Venetians occupied not only the Ionian islands but also various coastal points all around Southern Greece and Crete; the Knights of St John established themselves in Rhodes.

Two hundred-odd years later, in 1453, Constantinople fell to the Ottoman Turks under Mehmet II, who swiftly moved on to conquer Greece. By 1461 virtually the entire mainland was in their hands and was to remain so for some 400 years; Rhodes was taken in 1522 and Crete in 1661. Although in some places, such as the Southern Peloponnese and certain remote mountain areas, the Turks wielded only token power, Greeks regard the Turkish occupation as the darkest of their Dark Ages; their hatred and suspicion of Turkey stems from this period.

War of Independence
Greece officially declared its revolution against Ottoman rule in 1821, and the spread of philhellenism in Western Europe, which had begun during the Renaissance, ensured outside sympathy and support for its cause — most notably, of course, from Lord Byron. Britain, France and Russia combined to put pressure on the Ottomans to cede independence to a new 'Greek State' and, following the almost accidental Battle of Navarino in which much of the Turkish-Egyptian fleet was sent to the bottom of a Peloponnesean bay, the Turks agreed.

Greece regained the Peloponnese, a few islands and parts of what are now Beotia and Southern Epiros in the central part of the country. It also gained first a Bavarian King (Otto, or Othon), then a constitution, then a Danish King (George) to replace the deposed Othon. There followed a near-continuous struggle that lasted well into the 20th century to repossess all of the territory Greece had encompassed during the Byzantine period; not only Macedonia, the remainder of Southern Epiros (Northern Epiros is still part of Albania), Western Thrace and Crete, in which it succeeded, but also Asia Minor, in which it failed, the final disastrous blow being Turkey's sack of the Greek enclave of Smyrna (now Izmir) in 1922.

Twentieth Century
Meantime, important reforms at home, instigated by the statesman Eleftherios Venizelos, who came to power before World War I and aligned his country with Britain and France during that war, were interrupted by periods of political instability during which King George's successor, Constantine, was first deposed, then reinstated, then deposed again In 1935 his son, George II, was enthroned and Venizelos exiled to France, and in the following year General Metaxas became dictator.

World War Two, in which Greeks fought bravely against the occupying

The Country and its History

Axis forces, was followed by two bitter civil wars (for an idea of how bitter, read "Eleni" by Nicholas Gage, published by Collins and Fontana). Yet more political instability followed, but under the first premiership of Constantine Karamanlis huge strides were taken in restoring order and making economic progress: it was he who steered his country towards eventual membership of the European Community. But Karamanlis lost office in 1963 and the ensuing political confusion ended with the bloodless 'Colonels' revolution of 1967. This military regime, lasting over six years, failed to bring Greece any significant economic benefit and was itself overthrown by another, this time short-lived, military junta which nearly took Greece into war with Turkey over Cyprus.

From 1974, when the monarchy was abolished, until this volume went to press in November 1988, Greece has had but two Prime Ministers: a reinstated Karamanlis, followed by Andreas Papandreou leading a Socialist government. Its overall economy has made significant strides — currently being paid for by a period of austerity — and it is now a full member of the EEC. Despite threats to withdraw, it remains within NATO and there are even hopes that the age-old enmity with Turkey, latterly exacerbated by oil-exploration disputes, may be nearing its end.

The Erechtheion, Athens

Athens and Attica

Athens

City of Theseus and Pericles, wellspring of the political, philosophical and artistic ideals that have inspired the entire Western World and thus in a sense the progenitor of all we hold most dear; Athens, with Rome and Jerusalem, is one of the world's most emotive place names. Yet, whichever way it is approached — from the airport, the port of Piraeus or along the motorway from the north, the first impression is liable to be disappointing and it is essential to remember something of the recent history which has wiped so much of the illustrious past from the city's face. By Byzantine times Athens had already dwindled in importance to the ranks of a small provincial town and it was subsequently sacked by Slavs, fortified by Franks, briefly ruled by Florentines and finally taken by the Turks in 1456.

Turkish Rule
During the next four centuries Athens remained a backwater, almost forgotten by the rest of the world. A few churches were built, by permission of the Turks, who had fortified the Acropolis, converted the Parthenon into a mosque and the Propylaia into a gunpowder store — which exploded during a Venetian seige in 1687. After the

Athens and Attica

Turks had re-taken Athens, a few venturesome Western European scholars — and collectors of antiquities — began to take an interest in the shattered city, starting with Sir George Wheler in 1675. It was during the following century that Lord Elgin (and, to a lesser extent, the French Ambassador of that period) made their acquisitions, at least partly with the aim of saving the Parthenon treasures from further damage.

Independence and Development

After Athens became the capital of the newly-independent Greece in 1834, a new city was laid out below the Acropolis, the straggly village that surrounded its slopes and the remains of Hadrian's city alongside it, by German architects imported by Greece's first King, Othon (Otto of Bavaria). This was the Athens occupied by the Allies in the First World War and of the immediate post-war period, until the "castastrophe" of 1922 when over a million Greeks, expelled from Asia Minor, engulfed the city. Then it was that haphazard shanty towns sprang up almost overnight all around the capital to become the cores of today's ugly, sprawling suburbs.

The depredations both of World War II and the Civil War that followed it did not help, neither did the frenetic rebuilding during the impoverished years immediately afterwards. Land-rich, cash-poor families and small businesses feverishly turned their old houses and premises over to developers in return for some money in the bank to buy food and clothes, and the prospect of a jerry-built flat to live in or office to occupy when the new building was up, and neither they nor the city itself had the resources — let alone the foresight — even to consider such niceties as city-planning or building standards. Hence the principal shopping and commercial areas are still in the city-centre, sucking in ever increasing numbers of shoppers and commuters from the suburbs and adding to the congestion — and the pollution whose most important victim is the Parthenon itself.

This pollution, from traffic and from heating systems, has caused Athens to be almost perpetually shrouded in smog — the *nefos*. Curbing the number of vehicles entering the city centre (by the final digit on registration plates: odd numbers may circulate on odd-number dates, even numbers on even-number ones) has helped to an extent. What does not help is the city's once-peerless setting, ringed to landward by Mounts Parnes, Pentelis and Hymettos. Instead of providing a shapely frame, they are now as often as not barely visible, acting as a barrier that hinders the *nefos* from dispersing.

Right: The Erectheion before current restoration (top).
            The Acropolis (below).
Overleaf: Kapnikerea Church, Athens (top).
            The Tower of the Winds, Athens (below).

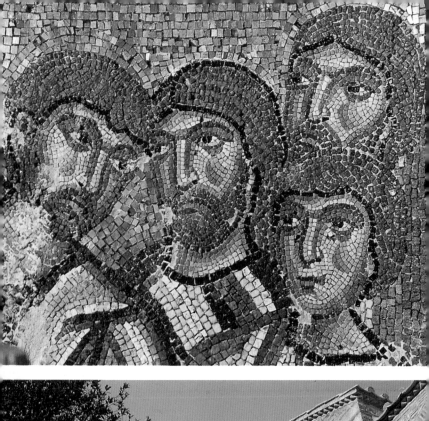

However, it is still possible most of the time to see, above the angular concrete mini-skyscrapers and the neon signs, the outlines of the temples on the Acropolis; the sharp peak of Mount Lykabettos with its whitewashed monastery, and the rounded swellings of the Pnyx (where the Assemblies met in ancient times), the Areopagus, the Mouseion and Nymphaeon hills.

Modern Athens
The heart of modern Athens is Syntagma (Constitution) Square with the Parliament Building (the former palace of King Othon) on its eastern side, the Grande Bretagne and King George Hotels flanked by two modern hotels, the Astir Palace and the NJV Meridien, to its north, and cafés and airline offices on the other two sides. To the north-west two wide streets, Stadiou and Panepistímiou, stretch towards Ommonia Square and the railway station, past the Academy, the University and National Library. Beyond Ommonia is Patissíon Street and the National Archaeological Museum. To the north-east, on the slopes of Lykabettos and bounded by Vasilissis Sophias Avenue, is the chic Kolonaki residential area where most of the embassies are, and also the Benaki, Byzantine and Goulandris Museums and the British and American Schools of Archaeology.

South-east of Syntagma are the National Gardens, prettily landscaped under the supervision of King Othon's wife, Amalia, and the Zappeion Gardens. They are bounded to the west by Amalias Avenue, to the south by Vassilis Olgas Avenue (south of which again are the Roman Olympian Zeus Temple and Hadrian's Arch), and the Stadium, and to the east by the exclusive Iroduou Attikou Street and the former palace of the deposed King Constantine and his immediate antecedents, now used by the President. The older, Plaka, quarter of the city, crawling up the Acropolis Hill, the Acropolis itself, and the remains of the Hellenistic city, lie to the south-west of Syntagma.

The Acropolis
Few can resist visiting the Acropolis first, open daily 0730 to 1930, shorter hours on Sundays and in winter. A road leads past the Theatre of Dionysos, (see below), and past the Roman Odeum of Herodus Atticus to the steep Roman path and stairway that winds up over the foundations of earlier cities past the Frankish-built Beulé gateway to the central opening of the massive Propylaia, designed by Mnesikles and built in the 5th century BC. To the south of it, almost jutting out over the hillside, stands the enchanting tiny Athena Niké temple,

Previous page: Bassae before current restoration (left). Monemvasia (right). Treasury of the Athenians, Delphi (below).
Left: Detail of mosaic at Nea Moni Hios (top). Monastery of Osios Loukas, near Delphi (below).

roughly contemporary with the Propylaia, and currently closed for restoration. The former Sacred Way led from the Propylaia across the central axis of the Acropolis, passing between the colossal bronze statue of Athena (only the base foundations remain), a row of lesser statue-bases and two sacred buildings that are now merely fragments. Visitors can however no longer pick their way among the stones attempting to identify these remains; to control today's throngs and restrict damage from (and possibly to) their feet, a broad concrete pathway, roped along both sides, now leads to the Parthenon, standing on the site of an earlier temple.

Parthenon
This peerless monument, built in Pericles' time, was used as a treasury rather than a place of worship and contained incalculable wealth. Its 46 Doric columns are cunningly varied to give an optical illusion of regularity; its sculptured friezes, metopes and pediments, by Phidias and his pupils (most of what remains of them are in museums, including the British Museum, and two of the pediment lions were removed by the Venetians in 1687 and now guard Venice's arsenal) were originally brightly painted. Phidias's gargantuan gold-plated statue of Athena was encrusted with jewels, and the ceiling in all probability was equally gaudily decorated: what we now see is a bleached, steamlined skeleton. We can only view it from a distance, moreover, and through scaffolding in places; the major restoration now in progress is likely to take longer than the original work of building it, which was probably 10 years.

Behind the Parthenon is the circular foundation stone of a Roman temple and the Parthenon Museum (due to give way to a new one by the mid-1990s) with a unique collection of Archaic sculpture from the 7th, 6th and early 5th centuries BC, all found on the Acropolis, as well as one of the Parthenon metopes and fragments of the frieze.

Erechtheion
Continuing round the periphery, there is a belvedere terrace with stunning views in clear weather, particularly at sunset, over central Athens towards Lykabettos and the mountains behind. Further round, at the centre of the northern edge of the rock, is the newly-restored Erechtheion, built alongside (and designed to succeed) the Old Temple of Athena which has now all but disappeared. Built on several levels just after the Parthenon, its interior is confusing; its best-known features are the beautiful Ionic columns along the North Portico and the Portico of the six so-called Caryatids (the originals of which have all now been replaced by copies to preserve them from deterioration).

Views of Acropolis
Opposite the Acropolis to the west is the Areopagos hill whose name, in Greek Ários Págos, derives from Ares, god of war. Here the original (noble) rulers of Athens once met to hold council, until they were

superseded by democracy and the democratic assemblies that were held on the Pnyx, rising above it to the south. On the slopes of the Areopagos are traces of Mycaenean tombs and an Early Helladic house, and tradition has it that St Paul preached here. The summit of the Pnyx (from which audiences nowadays watch the Acropolis *Son et Lumière* performances) is a huge man-made terrace. Behind it, on the slope of the Hill of the Nymphs, is the former Observatory; from the gardens around it is perhaps the most romantic view of the Acropolis, framed in greenery that hides the modern city. Completing this quartet of ancient hills is Philopappou, or Mouseion Hill, with the Roman monument of Philopappos topping it; here too is the theatre at which, in summer, the Dora Stratou company give nightly performances of Greek folk dancing and singing.

Theatres; Agora; Kerameikos

Below the Acropolis hill to the south are the restored Roman Theatre of Herod Atticus, where Festival of Athens performances take place, and the much older Theatre of Dionysos (open all day, except Tuesdays). This largely dates from the 4th century BC, though parts were restored by the Romans, whose chief legacies are the high-relief stone panels fronting the stage. The paving of the orchestra is set with a lozenge, marking the spot where the altar of Dionysos stood. It is a peaceful spot, shaded by pepper trees and overlooked, from the hillside, by a cave that once housed the Dionysos monument erected by a chorus leader, Thrasyllos; the cave was later converted to a Christian chapel, Panaghia Spiliotissa. Above it again are two Roman columns, also votives to Dionysos.

Agora

To the north of the Acropolis hill are the jumbled remains of the ancient Greek agora, spread over the tree-shaded hillside and for the most part little-visited. (It is open, as are the other monuments below, daily except Tuesdays until mid-afternoon). Marooned among the ruins is the charming 11th-century Byzantine church of Aghioi Apostoli, restored in 1956, but most visitors concentrate on just two sights in this area: the heavily-restored Stoa of Attalos, now a museum containing finds from the agora excavations, and the so-called Thission, or Temple of Hephaistos on the opposite edge of the site. This is the best-preserved of Athens' 5th-century BC Doric temples, not unlike the Parthenon but lacking the drama of a lofty situation.

Monastiraki

Just north of the ancient agora area (but getting out of the gates involves a roundabout walk) is Monastiraki Square, on Ermou Street, the heart of the flea market (now very touristy and *declassé*). It takes its name from the convent/monastery once attached to the 17th-century church in the centre of the square. Just off it, in a former Turkish mosque, are the Museum of Greek Popular Art (currently closed for restoration) and, adjoining it, the handsome Corinthian colonnade that is all that remains of Hadrian's Library.

Kerameikos

At the foot of Ermou Street, some way to the west, is the ancient cemetery of Athens, the Kerameikos (open daily except Tuesdays until mid-afternoon). It is one of the pleasantest spots in which to wander: green and agreeably untidy, and quiet despite the traffic roaring along the roads that border it. There are some fine Hellenistic *stelae* (funerary monuments) to admire on its hillocks and in the hollows, and the small adjoining museum displays delightful votives and children's toy figures, some dating back to the 8th century BC; gold jewellery and Roman glass, and more *stelae*.

Walking back east along Ermou street brings you eventually to Syntagma Square, skirting the lower reaches of the Plaka quarter at the foot of the Acropolis hill. Also on Ermou, and Metropóleos, just parallel with it, are two important 12th century churches, the Kapnikárea, and the Little Metropolis: tiny, with ancient panels that date back to the 4th century BC set into its outer walls, it stands in the shadow of the huge 19th century Big Metropolis (Cathedral).

Plaka Sights; Ommonia Square

The Plaka, spilling downhill from the foot of the Acropolis, has grown up from the Turkish village Byron found when he visited Athens in 1809. Now, although its streets still follow their ancient courses, dictated by the contours of the hill and linked by flights of steps, its houses are mostly of 19th century patrician origin, interspersed by modern ones. For a decade or more in the 1970s and early 1980s it became vulgarly commercialised and tawdry in the extreme but in recent years much effort and money has gone into cleaning the area up: restoring old houses, pedestrianising many of the streets, closing some of the worst tourist traps. Now it is again becoming pleasant to stroll in, and some of Athens' more charming smaller sights are to be found in its streets.

Roman Forum

At its western edge, almost bordering the ancient Greek agora, are the remains of the Roman Forum (open daily until mid-afternoon),. Its most striking monuments can both equally well be viewed from outside the fencing: a huge gateway of the 2nd century AD and, at the opposite end, an octagonal marble building, dating from the time of Julius Caesar and originally housing a hydraulic clock. It is known as the Tower of the Winds from the reliefs around its uppermost part, which represent the prevailing Athenian winds.

Museums; Churches

Higher up the hill, at the top of Panos Street, the Kanellópoulos Museum (open daily until mid-afternoon except on Tuesdays) houses in a 19th-century mansion a good, eclectic small collection of Byzantine ikons and crucifixes, ancient clay figurines, pots and bronzes. Close by is the little Metamorphósis church with its rounded dome, and beyond it the fine 19th-century former University building. Further west, the church of Aghioi Anargíri rises between tall cypresses above a convent wall, and further west again is the Lysikrátes Monument, a drum-shaped edifice of 334 BC. It is the sole survivor of a series of votive monuments erected along Trípodos Street in celebration of victories in the Dionysiac Games, all supporting the tripods *(trípodos)* awarded to winners. Just beyond it is the church of Aghia Ekaterini, dating back to the 13th century.

Kidathinaéon Street, downhill from the Lysikrates Monument, has two more small museums off it: the Museum of Traditional Greek Art, open every morning, and the Centre for Popular Arts and Traditions, open mornings and late afternoons, both closed on Mondays.

Hadrian's Arch; Temple of Zeus
Kidathináeon leads on downhill, the restaurants, boutiques and souvenir shops becoming thicker with every step, towards Amalias Avenue and the Zappeion Gardens; by bearing right at the end, you come to the two largest remnants of Roman Athens: Hadrian's Arch, flanking a noisy traffic junction, originally built in 131 AD to separate the old Greek and new Roman cities, and the 15 towering columns that remain of the Temple of Olympian Zeus (open daily until mid-afternoon).

Not far away, tucked into the southwest corner of the Zappeion Gardens where Amalias and Olgas Avenues meet, is a statue of Byron — the work of two French sculptors.

Commercial Centre
To the north of Ermou Street, Athinas Street bisects the teeming Athens food markets. Parallel to it, Aeolou Street, with its many shops and the little Aghia Irini square (church, and flower market) runs past. Kotzia Square, bounded by the Town Hall, Central Post Office and Bank of Greece buildings, where recent excavations have uprooted the trees to reveal a jumble of ruins, including 5th-century BC graves. Beyond it is Ommonia Square, heart of commercial Athens (métro station for Piraeus) with fountains at its centre. In the triangle formed by Aeolou and Stadiou Streets, on Klafthómonos Square, is the 11th century Byzantine church of Aghioi Theodoroi, oldest in Athens, small and dark. Aeolou Street, after it passes Ommonia Square, becomes Patission Street, and just off it to the east is Kanningos Square, named for George Canning, the British Foreign Secretary who in 1823 aligned Britain with the Greeks' independence struggle.

Archaeological and other Museums
A short way further north is the most important of all Greek museums,

the National Archaeological Museum (open daily, except Mondays, all day, shorter hours on Sundays and holidays).

Crammed with treasures, this museum would repay weeks of study. Its highlights, however (starting with the ground floor), are the Mycaenean antiquities in the first hall; the Archaic sculptures in the north wing, the bronze Poseidon statue in Room 15, the Classical votive sculptures in Room 17 and the funerary monuments next door, and the bigger sculptures in the new wing. There are more superb bronzes (small ones, mostly from Dodona) in the Karpanos Collection (Room 36) and (larger, Archaic ones) in Room 37. The south wing contains mainly Hellenistic and Roman sculptures; in the penultimate room (no. 32) is the jewellery in the Hélène Stathatos Collection. Upstairs are the magnificent pottery collections, the Coin Rooms, and the separate Thira collection of objects and beautiful, delicate frescoes excavated within the last 20 years on Thera, or Santorini, by the late Professor Marinatos, who unearthed a Minoan township destroyed in 1500 BC but preserved, like Herculaneum, by volcanic ash.

Other Museums
Other museums of importance inlude the Byzantine Museum at 22 Vassilisis Sophias Avenue (open daily, except Mondays, all day), a small but sumptuous collection housed in the 19th century villa built for the eccentric French-born Duchess of Plaisance. The Benaki Museum nearby, on the corner of Koumbari Street and Vassilisis Sophias (open daily except Tuesdays, until mid-afternoon) is a highly eclectic and magnificent welter of pictures, objects d'art and historical mementoes (including Byronic relics). Also nearby, at 4 Neofytou Street, is the newer Goulandris Museum (open daily, except Sundays and Tuesdays, until mid-afternoon). Its small collection of Cycladic and Ancient Greek Art, of which the enigmatic stone Cycladic figures are the highlights, is beautifully displayed and unequalled anywhere.

Kolonaki Square; Lykabettos
Up the hill from these is Kolonaki Square, heart of the Belgravia-Chelsea area of Athens, tree-shaded and lined with cafés (and the British Council headquarters). It rejoices, incidentally, in one of the few salubrious public lavatories in Athens, discreetly hidden among the trees of the square. From Kolonaki Square it is possible to climb up the steep, pretty streets to a winding path that leads through trees and past the chapel of Aghios Isidorou to the summit of Lykabettos and the 19th century church of Aghios Yeoryios. Alternatively, a funicular tunnels upward from the top of Ploutarchou Street, and there are marvellous views from the terraces at the summit.

First Cemetery
One other curiosity of Athens that should not be missed is the First Cemetery just above the Ilissos area. (Walking on the banks of the

Ilissos, now mostly covered over and often dry, was much favoured by Plato and other Athenian intellectuals). It is signposted from Vouliagmenis Street, which carries the bulk of city traffic to Athens Airport East Terminal and has a splendid array of massively carved tombs and monuments to the most celebrated Greeks and Grecophiles (including Schliemann, discoverer of Mikine, or Mycaenae) of the last two centuries.

Shopping
Leather and Fur
Athens is not an outstanding centre of fashion, nor even of fashion accessories, but there is a variety of attractive things to buy, particularly in the handicrafts field (the National Organisation of Greek Handicrafts, 9 Mitropóleos Street, Athens, displays the best of them and advises on where to buy). Furs, shoes and other leather goods are also worth looking at. The centre of the fur trade is Kastoria in Northern Greece but it is in the fur shops around Syntagma, along Philellinon, Ermou and Mitropóleos Streets that their best wares can be found. Their bases are tiny snippets and small skins skilfully pieced together into coats, hats, scarves, rugs, etc., sometimes looking surprisingly like the real, whole-skin articles and sometimes deliberately mosaic-patterned, but always quite reasonably priced. Leather, though not as fine as the Italian or Spanish, is also reasonable and bargains can be found in casual handbags and belts and also in sandals; look in Miaouli Street and Monastiraki.

Jewellery
Jewellery is another traditional craft deriving its inspiration from the designs of antiquity and of the Byzantine age. The smartest (and most expensive) jewellery shops are Ilias Lalaounis and Zolotas on Penepistímiou Street, just off Syntagma Square, with branches elsewhere; their jewellery ranks with Hermès scarves as social castemarks. There are plenty of very much cheaper, but still extremely attractive, pseudo-Zolotas baubles to be found, in the more modest jewellery shops around Syntagma and Ommonia Squares and also among the tourist junk in the larger souvenir shops.

The famous Greek worry beads, or *koumboloi*, can be bought very cheaply in the souvenir shops, but for something more original or of better quality (the big ones look very decorative on occasional tables, for instance) try the Koumboloi Boutique at 7 Zalakósta Street, just off Syntagma Square, or Mati at 20 Voukourestíou Street.

Other Crafts
Carpets are good buys, too, from the beautiful hand-woven ones sold by the Handicrafts Division of the National Welfare Organisation (head office, 6 Ipatias Street, Athens; branches at 24a Voukourestíou Street and 135 Vass. Sophias Avenue in Athens, and at the Danilia Village

on Corfu). All can be produced to order, down to the more modest soft, shaggy Flocati wool rugs, dyed in various colours but probably best in their natural off-white colour.

The popular hand-woven shoulder bags, peasant skirts and tunics, embroidery and Rhodian pottery can all be found in the souvenir shops; souvenirs that are both useful and decorative are the traditional long-handled copper coffee pots (holding enough for one or two cups of Turkish coffee, and very useful for serving sauces or gravy), and long meat skewers. The coppersmiths' shops along Iféstiou Street, off Monastiraki Square, are the best hunting-ground for these.

Flea Market
The Sunday Flea Market, also off Monastiraki Square, is more for tourist sightseeing than for sensational bargain buys (beware of anything offered as an antique) but some of the second-hand junk (including a huge subterranean second-hand bookshop) is amusing, and the shops behind the flea market stalls along Pandróssou and Ploutonos Streets are useful for more conventional shopping on weekdays. For books and maps go to Eleftheroudakis, 4 Nikis Street, or to Pantelidis, 9 Amerikis Street, or the American Bookshop, 23 Amerikis Street, or to The Bookstall, 6-10 Har. Trikoupi, off Panepistimiou. Bookshops, incidentally, tend to open at different hours from other shops, sometimes not opening at all on Saturdays. Newspapers, including the very informative English language *Athens Daily News,* and foreign papers are found at the street kiosks.

Restaurants; Cafés; Hotels
Even those who go to Athens on a package deal should avoid arrangements that confine them to the hotel dining room for both main meals, and give themselves a chance to sample local food. There are scores of restaurants in Athens, since Greeks themselves are inveterate eaters-out but, as a great many of the nicest are only open in the evenings, the best idea is to eat at the hotel at midday (and then take a siesta, as the Greeks do). Remember, too, that Greeks eat late, especially in Athens: restaurants do not start to get busy until 2100 hours or later, though recent energy-saving regulations impel them to close at about 0200. Prices are still reasonable: even at the smarter places, three courses with wine are unlikely to exceed £12 except when there is music or some sort of floor show. Three typical unpretentious Plaka restaurants (open at lunchtime too) are Plátanos on Diogenos Street, near the Tower of the Winds, Yerani ("Geranium") on Trípodos Street, and Ta Bakalaraika, 41 Kidathineon Street, specialising in crisp-fried cod with garlic sauce. Most of those with music are very touristy but Xynos, 4 Angelou Geronda Street, one of the oldest Plaka tavernas (guitar music, evenings only, booking essential), still has an authentic feel. In the Syntagma/Kolonaki areas the Corfu at 6 Kriezótou Street (open at lunchtime) is reliable if unadventurous;

44

the Kentrikon, at 3 Kolokotroni, in a quiet arcade, has the atmosphere of a provincial *taverna*; Yerofínikas, 10 Pindárou Street (also open midday), is excellent, chic and expensive. Midway between Syntagma and Ommonia, the Ideal is old-established and reliable. Behind the Archaeological Museum, Kostoyannis at 37 Zaimi Street (evenings only, booking recommended) specialises in a huge array of starters followed by a typical Graeco-Turkish main dish and fruit. More international is the Dionysos, 43 Rov. Gali, opposite (and with fine views of) the Acropolis.

Cafés

Cafés, pastry shops and bars abound, the latter mainly in hotels (the smartest being that of the Grande Bretagne). Most of Syntagma is lined with cafés, all with tables in the centre of the square in summer. Just off it, on Panepistímiou Street, are the two most traditional bar-café-cum-pastry-shops, Floka's and Zonars. Both do excellent cakes to take away. The Kolonaki Square cafés are all popular with Athenian society people, but less peaceful than the Syntagma cafés, thanks to the proximity of the traffic. For a nice locale on a fine evening, there is nowhere better than the big open-air café next door to the Zappeion building in the Zappeion Gardens. For something authentically Athenian, try Krinos, 87 Eolou Street, where housewives fortify themselves with *loukoumádes* (deep-fried puffs of batter, drenched in honey) after doing their marketing.

Nightlife

Chatting and watching the world go by from a café table is the traditional form of Athenian evening entertainment, but for a special evening out look for places with the typically Greek *bouzoukia,* music that is at the same time both rhythmic, stirring and yet plaintive. They wax and wane a bit according to fashion and who is currently singing where, but among the more reliable, old-established Plaka tavernas that offer live music and dancing are Vrachos in Adrianou Street, Kalokerinós in Kekropos Street, and Palaiakritikou and Mostrou, both in Mnisikleous Street. Entrance is free to all of these, but the first drink will cost around 1,000 or more drachmas and subsequent ones only slightly less. Discothèques are more proliferous nowadays than of yore, both in the big hotels and elsewhere. For international-style dinner-show-and-dancing consult the weekly listings publication, *This Week in Athens.*

For theatres, cinemas, *Son et Lumière* and other entertainment, see *This Week in Athens.* The *Athens Daily News* also carries information about entertainments.

Hotels

For those not on a package deal, the modern Astir Palace and NJV Meridien, or the venerable Grande Bretagne (all on Syntagma Square) head my list in the de luxe category. The Amalia and the Attica Palace, both just off Syntagma, follow; both take better-class package tours. For the more impecunious traveller my suggestions are the Minerva, just off Syntagma Square at 3 Stadiou Street; the Parthenon, at 6 Makri; and the Acropolis View at 10 Wemster, off Rov. Gali (both south of the Acropolis), and Clare's House, at 24 Sorvolou Street near the First Cemetery. For connoisseurs of real Greek simplicity, Fivos at 12 Petta Street, Plaka, is recommended, likewise the elderly Royal, 44 Mitropóleos Street. For the names, addresses and prices of other hotels, pensions and apartments, both in Athens and elsewhere in Greece, the Chamber of Hotels of Greece (24 Stadiou Street, Athens) publishes an annual directory listing places according to their official classifications, and the *Greek Travel Pages* also carries a wide cross-section of names.

Attica: South-west and West

Piraeus

Originally an island, Piraeus is a hilly promontory to the south-west of Athens which has been its port since Themistocles first decided the city should have a fleet in the early 5th century BC. He surrounded it by massive fortifications and started building the famous Long Walls, protecting the way to Athens, which were completed by Pericles later. Nearly all traces of both have disappeared but a small section of fortifications can be seen at the mouth of the Zea harbour, on the eastern side (known formerly as the Pasalímani).

Harbours

Atki Miaoulis, flanking the main harbour, is on the western side: from here the inter-island ships sail and the quayside is lined with numerous cafés, the bus station, the métro station (direct to Ommonia Square, Athens, in 20 minutes), the market, the passenger terminal, the shipping and port offices and the Customs House, all dominated by the huge Town Hall with its clock. A ridge, along which runs the shady Vasiléos Konstantinou Avenue, divides this commerical half of Piraeus from the more fashionable eastern half, sloping away from the ancient Munychia hill (now the Kastella quarter, currently becoming markedly gentrified and with a café at the summit). Below it are two crescent-shaped harbours where yachts crowd the fishing boats: Zea, and the smaller Tourkolímano, or Microlímano, with the Yacht Club on its southern promontory.

Piraeus has no mythological associations and little architectural merit, but it teems with raucous Mediterranean port-town life and colour, and there are worse places in which to kill a few hours between island connections. Next to the ruined Hellenistic Theatre of Zea, just above the harbour of the same name, on Trikoupi Street, is a small

Archaeological Museum (open daily until mid-afternoon) the principal exhibit of which is a life-sized Archaic bronze statue of Apollo, cast in 520 BC: the oldest large bronze figure in the world and superbly intact. There are also some good *stelae* of the 4th century BC. The walk along the eastern end of the promontory, on a road supported in places by Kronon's Walls (a restoration of the Themistoclean ones) parts of which are occasionally visible, is pleasant in the evenings: it ends by the Naval College at an ancient tomb popularly called that of Themistocles.

Restaurants
Some 20 fish restaurants, open-air in summer, encircle the Turkolímano: they are all much of a muchness as far as standards go. The fish is excellent, and prices vary with the type and weight of fish chosen. *Kaffeneions* abound, and *bouzoukia tavernas.*

Salamis; Daphní; Elefsis

Salamis
Shipyards and naval dockyards line most of the coast west of Athens as far as Perama and beyond to Skaramangas. As well as launches from Piraeus, car ferries from Perama cross to the island of Salamis, famous as the scene of the great naval battle of 480 BC in which the Persian fleet under Xerxes was decimated by the Greeks under Themistocles. Athenians go to swim off its farther shore in summer and it has good fish restaurants; otherwise Salamis is of little interest to any but hard-core Grecophiles.

Daphní
Near the shores of the Bay of Eleusis (pronounced Elefsis), which the north flank of Salamis almost encloses, are two of the most important sights in the Athens area: Daphní and Elefsis itself, both off the same main road leading west out of Athens. The 11th century monastery of Daphní (open daily until mid-afternoon) is one of the most important Byzantine monuments in the country. It lies at the edge of the pine-woods where the Wine Festival is held each September, and its great glory is its mosaics, particularly the Pantokrator on the vault of the dome.

Ruins of Elefsis
Some fifteen kilometres (eight miles) further on, past the reedy salt lagoons of Koumoundourou, and shrouded in the fumes of the fast-expanding industrial town and adjacent cement-works, is the ancient sacred site of Elefsis (open daily except Tuesdays until mid-afternoon) even more poignant perhaps in its ugly setting. Here the cult of Demeter, mother of Persephone and goddess of fertility, was practised, part of the rites (mysteries, connected with the legend of Persephone's descent to the Underworld and her eventual return, coinciding with winter and spring), being held in secret. The ruins, most of them

dating from the 4th and 5th centuries BC, with later restorations, but on a site whose association with the goddess goes back at least 1,000 years earlier, are extensive but hardly impressive. There is a good view of them from the terrace of the modern church at their edge, and the entrance *propylaea* and central *Telesterion* (Temple of Demeter) are the most interesting parts. There is also a small museum.

History of Elefsis: 1200-1800 AD
The history of Elefsis after the cult of the old gods died is worth summarising here; it is almost a microcosm of the history of many an ancient Greek site. I am indebted for this information to Aristide Metheniti, whose family came from Elefsis and who has researched the subject exhaustively and published a book on it (in Greek).

Abandoned for centuries, its partial reoccupation started in 1205 when a Frankish conqueror took possession of the area after the Fourth Crusade. Franks were succeeded by Spaniards and, at the end of the 14th century, by Florentines who imported Orthodox Greeks from what is now Albania to guard their Attica kingdom, manning a line of village frontier-posts running roughly from Halkis to Corinth.

They were allowed freedom of worship and to bear arms and they stayed in the neighbourhood following the Turkish occupation in 1456, when Elefsis came under the rule of the Turkish governor of Athens. They did not live at the site itself; in 1676 Sir George Wheler, who saw the famous statue of Ceres/Demeter there (it is now in the Fitzwilliam Museum in Cambridge), reported that the villagers went to the mountains each night, for fear of pirates.

Elefsis: 1800-1988 AD
A century later, Richard Chandler, another English visitor, got a permit from the Turkish governor to study the site, giving him a tobacco-box in return. Shortly thereafter, the Turks started to allow a few favoured Greeks to buy land and settle at Elefsis, and it is reasonable to suppose that they financed their transactions by selling smaller antiquities. The goddess's statue, however, was still *in situ* in 1801 "buried to her ears" when Edward Clarke, also English, got permission (in return for a telescope this time) to buy it from the villagers — who even then lit candles before it for the sake of their crops.

"Albanian" Greeks were among the first to bear arms against the Turks in the War of Independence and, when they returned to their villages after it was over, their new status as freedom heroes led them to have their sons educated for the professions rather than continue as peasants. Later, these sons and their sons started the first small industries, producing resin, soap from the residue of olive oil — and the cement that today has taken over the entire area. In the 1880s the first professional excavations began at the site and the new railway brought visitors to look at it. It was the start of a halcyon period that ended in 1922 when the "catastrophe" of Smyrna (Izmir) took place and thousands of Greeks fled from Turkey.

Aristide Metheniti's mother told him of ships that sailed up the coast, arbitrarily putting ashore at likely places groups of refugee Smyrna Greeks; at Elefsis they had to be housed in the church at first until they could build huts for themselves. They were, however, far more sophisticated than the local inhabitants; even their huts were scrupulously kept and planted about with gardens and gradually their energy and resourcefulness transformed the small village alongside the ancient site into the heavily industrialised township it is today.

Thriasian Plain

The Thriasian Plain, behind Elefsis, is bounded on the north by Mount Parnes with the chapel of Aghia Trias near its summit (not accessible, being a military zone). To the east are rudimentary ski-facilities and the top station of a cable-car that brings visitors up to the Grand Hotel Mount Parnes (casino). Below them, overlooking the plain, is the charming 14th century convent of Moni Kleistón, and on the road that winds down from it towards Athens is the village of Filí, close to the ruins of the ancient fortress of Phyle, and with several small *tavernas* that are popular with Athenians.

Eléftherai and Egósthena

Just after Elefsis, the old road for Thebes branches off to the right and climbs towards the mountains, scattered with old watchtowers, that separate Attica from Boeotia (see under Central Greece). Beyond the village of Oinio is a fork, the inland arm leading to the great ramparts of the 4th century BC fortress of Eléftherai, which guarded Athens and Attica from the north. The left fork continues to the eastern-most extremity of the Gulf of Corinth and the even more massive and better-preserved fortress of Egósthena, also late 4th century BC, rising above the Gulf and miles of olive groves. The small modern seaside resort of Porto Germanó, beyond it, is popular with Greeks and has a couple of good restaurants.

Attica: The South Coast

Athens to Sounion

The coast road south from Athens goes first through the suburb of Nea Smyrni and joins the sea at Faliron, near the racecourse and the Military Cemetery (graves of British and Commonwealth soldiers killed in World War II). This formerly rather seedy area has been extensively redeveloped: a huge stadium, used for shows and spectaculars as well as sports, stands on reclaimed land near the sea; there is a new marina and other, more serious-looking, nautical installations. If the beach does not look tempting there is a public swimming-pool. Inland and south of it the buildings (mostly apartments with some hotels and shops) stretch uninterruptedly, separated from the seashore by the six-lane highway, through Palaion Faliron, Kalamaki, Alymos and Ellenikón (where the airport is) to Glyfadha.

Glyfadha

This is the first of the more popular resorts, with dozens of package-tour hotels sitting almost beneath the flight-path of aircraft landing at or taking off from Ellenikón. (There are plans, almost hoary with age, to move the airport inland to the east, near Spata). At the heart of Glyfadha is a recognisable descendant of the village *plateia* around which it has grown up, and near the Antonópoulos Hotel (q.v.) are the remains of an early Christian Basilica (St Paul is said to have landed here). Numerous marinas edge the reclaimed land along the shore and there are several good fish restaurants: Diónysos, with a garden; the restaurant of the Antonópoulos Hotel and the eternally popular and crowded Psarópoulos. In the square, a *taverna* serves *tiropitta* (cheese pie) and spit-roasted chicken.

Coastal Resorts

Glyfadha runs smoothly in to Voula where there is a public beach run by the National Tourist Office, and Voula into Kavouri, on a small peninsula with the main road consequently running behind it. Much of it is in single private ownership that has spared it from over-development. Vouliagmeni is the smartest resort on the coast with another National Tourist Office beach; the waters of its bay are infiltrated by sulphur springs and thus held to be particularly healthy, though recent reports suggest that many other beaches along this coast are heavily polluted. Many hotels here, of all classes, plus a magnificent yacht marina and a sailing school. Inland of the main road and less visited except by connoisseurs, is Vouliagmeni Lake, a volcanic crater fed by mineral springs that are 8-10° hotter than the sea and beneficial for rheumatism. There are changing rooms, flowery terraces, and a treatment centre (staffed July-September only). Across the humpy, three-pronged Vouliagmeni promontory, in fact the end of the Hymettos mountain range, is Varkiza, yet another resort, beyond which the development starts to thin out, with private villas visible below the corniche road and, so far, fewer hotels. Lagonissi, Anavissos, Saronida and Legrena are all developing resorts on this much-indented, mostly rocky coast between Vouliagmeni and Sounion, at the peninsula's tip.

Sounion

The bay below this steep headland is rapidly being built over with hotels and thick with day-visitors in summer, which rather mar the incredibly dramatic effect of the veined-marble Temple of Poseidon which crowns the levelled acropolis at its summit (and is now roped off, to keep the crowds back). Built about the middle of the 5th century

BC on the foundations of an earlier temple, it commands magnificent views over the Aegean. Traditionally these are finest at sunset; the prudent visitor will therefore conclude that sunrise is a quieter time or at any rate 0900, when it opens. (It closes at sunset). Byron, who wrote some memorable lines there, carved his name on one of the pillars.

Attica: South and East

Around Hymettos and Pentelis

Inland of and above the city to the east looms the smooth outline of Mount Hymettos, almost treeless but covered with herbs and aromatic shrubs which give the famous honey its distinctive flavour. A road leads to the top, with stupendous views in clear weather; at its foot is the 11th century monastery of Kesseriani, with later frescoes, a favourite Sunday outing for Athenians; further up is the pretty, half-ruined little Astériou monastery, also 11th century, from which a path leads down again to a Byzantine church, Aghios Ionannis Theólogos. In the foothills to the north, between Hymettos and Pentelis, and reached by the underground railway from central Athens, the airy fashionable Athens garden suburbs of Maroussi and Kifissia (this latter with a number of good hotels and restaurants) and the Goulandris Museum of Natural History (open daily, except Fridays, until early afternoon) with an excellent herbarium containing thousands of varieties of Mediterranean plants. Beyond Kifissia to the north, cradled between Pentelis and Parnes is Varybobi (golf course) and Tatoi, or Dhekelia, where the former royal summer residence is. On the eastern flank of Pentelis, reached from Athens through Halandris, is the convent of Moni Penteli, founded in the 16th century. Just south of it is the 19th century Rododafnis Palace, built for the French-born Duchess of Plaisance, an ardent, if eccentric, supporter of the cause of Greek independence. Now restored, its courtyard is used for concerts in summer. Above it, near the summit of Pentelis, are the ancient quarries from which the famous Pentelic marble was hewn.

The Messogheia to Lavrion

The red-soil plain to the east of Hymettos, the Messogheia, is extremely fertile and beautiful, rich with vines that yield the excellent Messogheia *retsina*. The villages of Peanía, Drossia and Liopesi, famous as the birthplace of Demosthenes, have dozens of good *tavernas* where it is pleasant to sit in the open and eat spit-roasted young lamb in the early spring. Peanía also boasts Attica's only sizeable cave: Koutouki. Beyond it is Pikermi where in 1870 an aristocratic English party returning from Marathon was kidnapped by brigands, who eventually murdered four of them. The village is now being built up with the expensive country retreats of pop stars and media folk.

Athens and Attica

North of it is the wealthy Daou-Penteli Monastery. Markópolou, to the south, is big and busy and famous for its bread, which the chauffeurs of rich Athenians were at one time sent to buy — until their local bakers realised the desirability of baking "country bread" themselves. Markópolou also has a tiny 11th century church that has recently been well restored; the frescoes are 16th century.

Lavrion

From Markópolou a road runs south through fruit groves and vineyards to Lavrion (also reachable by road from Sounion, by way of some singularly unremarkable new coastal development). Now an unappealing industrial town, Lavrion is not entirely devoid of interest. In antiquity, its silver mines provided the finance with which Athens built the ships that defeated the Persians at the Battle of Salamis in 480 BC, and those professionally interested can still visit an ancient mine (apply to Metallourghiki Eteria Lavrion). The less committed can see one from the outside, and the oldest, least-visited, theatre in Attica as well, by turning right just north of Lavrion to Thorikos. The theatre (visible from the main road and unfenced) is unusual in that it is faintly elliptical in shape; beside it is the (barred) entrance to an ancient silver mine and, below this, a heavily restored complex of troughs, level spaces and gutters in which silver and rock were separated in running water.

East Coast

Vravrona

Following minor roads up the east coast of Attica reveals much unlovely development, most of it the inexpensively-built summer houses of Athenians. The once-charming resort of Porto Rafti, from which Athenian treasure ships used to sail to the sacred island of Delos, is all but engulfed by it. Northwards again, a large new hotel has been unfortunately sited to overlook one of the loveliest sites in all Greece: the Temple of Artemis at Brauron (Vravrona).

According to a legend related by Euripides, it was founded by Iphigenaia, daughter of Agamemmnon, who had, with the goddess's help, escaped being sacrificed in return for a fair wind for Troy. After returning from exile in Tauris, where she had apparently slain a bear which was mauling a child — Artemis was the protector of bears — she built the temple, dedicating it to Artemis and filling it with small girls, known as "Bears".

Only excavated some 30 years ago by Professor Marinatos, discoverer of the Minoan town on Santorini, the 5th century BC sanctuary (open daily until mid-afternoon) is approached by the oldest bridge in Greece, crossing the tiny stream that was once fed by the sacred courtyard fountain. A fine colonnade is standing, part of what once surrounded the courtyard; the base of the temple is alongside. The museum displays some beautiful votive child-statuettes, including a rare Archaic one in wood, vases, and touching personal objects.

Rafina and Marathon
More haphazard development scars the coast to the north, though Loutsa is a comparatively mature and agreeable-looking resort, guarded by an islet bearing two sugar-lump convents (for the nuns' summer use) and a lighthouse. Rafina is a pleasant, workaday fishing- and ferry-port; it has a row of good fish-restaurants along its quay and car-ferries ply from there to Andros, Tinos, Mykonos, Naxos, Paros and Syros. North again, past yet more development, the Plain of Marathon is larger now than it was in ancient times, or in Byron's, but still overlooked by mountains. There, in 490 BC, an Athenian force used sophisticated military tactics to defeat a vastly bigger Persian army and the messenger running non-stop to the capital with the news fell dead with exhaustion on arrival; hence the name of the modern race. What there is to see is the Mound, or Soros, a barrow (open daily until mid-afternoon) raised in honour over the bodies of the 192 Athenians killed in the battle. A short way further north is a Helladic cemetery, excavated within the past 15 years, with tombs going back to 2000 BC, and a small museum (open until mid-afternoon except on Tuesdays) of finds from the tombs of both this and another nearby ancient cemetery. A smaller barrow in the area, near the village of Vrana, covers the graves of men from Plataia in Beotia, who also died at the Battle of Marathon.

The long and barely-developed beach at Shinias, backed by pine-woods, has a few cafés at its southern end.

Temple at Ramnous
Beyond Marathon, a minor road winds across fields in a north-easterly direction to the rather sparse remains of the Temple of Nemesis at Ramnous, dating from the late 5th century BC (open daily until mid-afternoon). Nemesis was the "fair" goddess, weighing up good against bad fortune. Her Doric temple and the colossal statue of her, mentioned by Pausanias, and the nearby, older temple of her sister-goddess Themis, are now merely scattered fragments, but the site, overlooking the sea and the shores of Euboea opposite, and nearly always wonderfully deserted, is one of the most romantically-placed in Attica.

Amphiáreio Sanctuary
Inland, the artificial reservoir of Marathon Lake lies in a plain liberally peppered with vestiges of prehistoric habitation. A minor road snakes northward from it and from Marathon, through Grammatikó and Karpandríti and the shady hills beyond to Kalamos. Just below it, on a sharp bend in the road, is the Amphiáreio Sanctuary (opening hours as for Ramnous). This is another of the least-visited and most delightful spots in Attica, on the slopes of a plane- and pine-clad gully with a

stream trickling through it. The waters were said to be curative and Amphiáreios himself, a 4th century BC King of Argos and a seer, was also a healer. The easily decipherable ruins thus comprise bath-houses, sanatoria and living quarters for those taking the cure as well as a temple and one of the prettiest little theatres imaginable. At Aghioi Apostoli, on the coast immediately east of Amphiáreion, tourist development is taking place; from Skala Oropos, on the site of ancient Oropos, to the north of it, ferries go to Eretria on Euboea.

Kastro Pylos, Peloponnese

The Peloponnese and Argo-Saronikos

Approaching the Peloponnese

Athens to Corinth

After Elefsis the main highway to Corinth cuts as straight a course as possible through the hills bordering the Saronic Gulf. Megara, a sprawling white town between two low hills (only a fountain remains from its past), is just north of the road. The old road to Corinth, following more nearly the path of antiquity, lies below the motorway, curling along and above the shore, through pine trees, skirting Kineta and Aghioi Theodori, both with thickening tourist development, and joining the new road just before the Canal. It is full of legendary associations, but it is sometimes hard to identify where the great hazards of antiquity lay, since so much terrain has been altered in the making of the new road. At the narrow pass, where the two roads run close together, known as the Kaki Scala (Evil Steps), the tyrant Skiron was wont to kick travellers into the sea after robbing them — until he was in his turn sent over the edge by Theseus. Near Aghioi

55

Theodori, Theseus slew the man-eating sow Phaea.

Loutraki Spa

Just before the Corinth Canal, a road forks to the right for Loutraki, a pleasant, well-matured and lively spa town (pop. c. 7000) noted for its delicious and healthy waters, fronted by a long fine-pebble beach. Flower-planted, with a cheerful main square and promenade, it has plenty of good hotels.

Heraion of Perahora

Beyond it the road winds through pinewoods and over the foothills of the Yerania mountains to the village of Perahora, inland, and then leads down again past a large lagoon and a clutch of *tavernas* to the tip of the promontory and the poetically sited Heraion of Perahora (unfenced). The ruins, sloping down to a tiny horseshoe-shaped harbour, are almost always deserted and include the foundations of an 8th century BC temple of Hera Limenia, of a later temple, stoa and altar, and a well-preserved Hellenistic cistern with steps leading into it, all dominated by a lighthouse; the whole area during the course of its pre-World War II excavations was beautifully described by Dilys Powell in 'An Affair of the Heart'.

Corinth Canal

Back at the Isthmus, one crosses the Corinth Canal. Between the clutter of road side cafés, the first turning to the left leads to the scattered village of Isthmia, from which an old-fashioned chain-ferry still operates across the canal. As well as the ruins of the classical sanctuary where the Isthmian games were held, a new museum displays finds from it, notably some glass mosaics recovered from sunken packing cases. (Both are open daily until mid-afternoon). It was near here that Theseus encountered and overcame yet another bully who plagued the travellers of antiquity, Sinis the Pine-Bender. Further south along the coast, which is gradually becoming built up with hotels but has stunning views across the Saronic Gulf, the ruins of the ancient port of Kenchrai lie offshore just before Loutra Elenis. The road continues south, above the sea, and eventually brings you to Epidavros.

Corinth

Back on the main road, modern Corinth (pop. c. 22,500), apart from its water's edge situation with pleasant *tavernas* both on the front and near the bus station in the town centre, is of little interest. One can skirt it via the main road and turn off a few kilometres later for Ancient Corinth, which is signposted, and the village of Old Corinth beside it. Open daily all day, this city where Jason and Medea spent three years is one of the most engrossing sites in all Greece. Wonderfully perched on a rocky plateau below the massive peak of Acro-Corinth, it has ruins of successive Byzantine, Frankish, Venetian and

Turkish fortifications, and a staggering view. Sitting strategically at the inner end of the Corinthian Gulf, Corinth's riches and maritime power date from the 7th-8th centuries BC for, even before the canal existed, seamen preferred to winch their ships across the isthmus than to face the dangers of circumnavigating the Peloponnese. Corinth was also noted for its hedonism and licentiousness: both before and after being taken by the Romans in 146 BC, its affluent *hetirae*, or courtesans, were a byword. They were of course still much in evidence during St Paul's eighteen-month sojourn in the city.

Ancient Corinth

The focal point of the ruins is the Doric Temple of Apollo, built in the 6th century BC and one of the oldest in Greece. It is slightly raised, and one thus gets a good view from it of the rest of the ruins around it, some of them Roman. They well repay a thorough prowl: along the Lechaeon Way, through the ruined Propylaia, stopping at the much-remodelled Fountain of Peirene caused by the tears Peirene shed for her son. Circling the Agora clockwise, past the Julian Basilica (formerly law-courts) and innumerable shop precincts, brings you to the Fountain of Glauke, Jason's second wife, into which Jason flung himself after donning a poisoned cloak given to him by Medea. Immediately beside is the museum, open the same hours as the site but closed on Tuesdays; its terracotta vases and Roman statuary are particularly interesting.

Corinth to Nafplion

A new highway across the Peloponnese, from Corinth south westward past Tripolis and Megalopolis towards Messini, is under construction and will eventually relieve congestion on the much prettier but narrow old one. This runs through orange and lemon groves and a succession of small villages, crossing and re-crossing the railway line and passing the scant, though signposted, ruins of ancient Kleone.

Nemea

The hills close in towards the Dervenakia Pass but, just before it (opposite a tree-shaded *taverna* complex, and a kiosk from which the excellent Nemea wines can be bought), is a side road to Ancient Nemea. This enchanting site open daily, except Tuesdays, until mid-afternoon, lies in a vine-planted valley beyond the modern village of the same name. It has recently been subjected to further excavations by the University of Berkeley, California, who unearthed many of the installations associated with the Nemean Games, including a bath-house, athletes' lodgings etc. The games were founded by Herakles, after he slew the Nemean lion, in honour of his father, Zeus, and the remains of the Temple of Zeus dominate the site, three of its slim Doric columns still towering above the cypress trees. A discreetly sited new museum, American donated, contains models of the site as it was in the 4th century BC and a rich collection of finds.

The Peloponnese and Argo-Saronikos

Citadel of Mycaenae

After the Dervenakia Pass the landscape opens out again into the beautiful plain of Argos. On a low hill overlooking it, but itself barely visible, is the massive, sombre citadel of Mycaenae (Mikine), reached from the village of Fiktiá (open all day every day). Occupied since earliest times (legendarily founded by Perseus) Mycaenae reached its zenith between 1400 and 1100 BC and gave its name to an entire civilisation. It was first excavated in 1874 by Schliemann, the amateur archaeologist whose decisions on exactly where to dig were made by careful reading of the accounts of Homer. Outside the citadel are numerous *tholoi,* or tombs, of which the most visited are the 13th century BC so-called Tomb of Agamemnon ("Treasury of Atreus"), the best preserved example of the "beehive" style; the tomb of Clytemnestra, and the earlier tomb of Aegisthus. Other tombs scattered over the area are of even earlier date and there are several excavated houses and a grave circle.

The entrance to the walled citadel, or acropolis, is by the famous Lion Gate, surmounted by a huge triangular stone carved with the reliefs of two lions facing inwards towards a column. To the right of the steep path up to the palace is the Royal Cemetery (the treasures it yielded are in the Athens museum), enclosed by concentric rings of huge stone slabs and containing six shaft graves; beyond this are the excavations of several houses. The Palace, crowning the acropolis, was built around a central court; the bases of columns and of many of the dividing walls are easily discernible. Below that to the south-east is the so-called Little Palace and beyond this again is the entrance (down steep underground steps, torch necessary) to the subterranean cistern. West of that are the remains of the Postern Gate, contemporary with the Lion Gate. Try to visit the site early and avoid the crowds.

Argos

After leaving Mycaenae and its adjacent cluster of modern *tavernas* and guest houses (even the famous Belle Hélène, where so many archaeologists lodged and supped, is now completely modernised), a minor road leads to the Heraion of Argos (also reachable from Argos itself). The remains of this unfenced Archaic and Classical sanctuary lie on three man-made terraces hewn from a mountain spur and are rather unjustly ignored. The buildings, built between the 7th and late 5th centuries BC, are in themselves far from uninteresting, and are also marvellously placed for gazing over the cypress-spiked plain down past Argos to the sea. Just south of it, also signposted, is Dhendra, whose tombs yielded many Mycaenean treasures now in the Athens and Nafplion museums.

Argos itself (pop. c. 20,000), held to be the oldest town in Greece, was razed during the War of Independence and rebuilt somewhat insensitively. It is full of legendary associations: here lived Danaos and his fifty daughters who married and then murdered the fifty sons of his brother Aegyptos, and were punished by being set for evermore to pour water into a bottomless well. It was an important city, ruled by Diomedes at the time of the Trojan War, but today all that remains is a steep, broken theatre, an *agora* and the shell of some Roman baths, all south of the town on a craggy slope topped by a Frankish castle. The modern town if you can beat the one-way system and penetrate it, has a thriving market, good *tavernas*, inexpensive hotels and *kaffeneions*, most of them around the *plateia* and the modern church at its centre. The little museum (open daily, except Tuesdays, until mid-afternoon) contains some early pottery and funerary items, Roman mosaics from the baths, and a fine 8th century BC suit of armour.

Tiryns
At Argos, signposts indicate the old road to Nafplion (Nauplio) and the Argolid peninsula. About 4 kilometres (2½ miles) short of Nafplion, on a small hill, rise the gigantic walls of the Mycaenean fortress of Tiryns, birthplace of Herakles. A ramp leads up to the gateway and into the first courtyard; the many-roomed palace complex opens off this to the south, ending in a colonnaded courtyard with a round hearth, or altar, which in turn gives onto the palace forecourt. The most impressive feature of Tiryns is, of course the elephantine grey walls which Homer and Pindar both mention; the galleries that lead through them, their walls polished to a sheen by the passage of hundreds of thousands of people; the casemates built into them, and the hidden stairway that descends, within one of the bastions, to the Postern Gate.

Nafplion
Nafplion, watched over by a sheer rocky acropolis topped by the vast Venetian fortress of Palamidi, is one of the most agreeable tourist centres in Greece, an excellent centre for the Eastern Peloponnese, with numerous hotels, restaurants, *kaffeneions* and tourist shops. Below the Palamidi fortress (open daily, all day, fine views from the bastions), down a precipitous flight of steps and along the rocky ridge known as Acronafplion, are the remains of three other fortresses called respectively the Castle of the Greeks, the Castle of the Franks and the Castello Torrione; the luxury Xenia Palace bungalow-hotel lies within them, complementing the older Xenia hotel, below the Torrione, and the Amphitrion, on the waterfront, now also part of the Xenia group. From here the city slopes downhill to the quaysides to north and west, of which the Akti Miaoulis is the liveliest, looking out to the Bourdzi island fortress. Beyond the western mole is a small beach.

Syntagma Square is the heart of the old town, briefly in the last century Greece's capital, and graced with some pleasant and carefully preserved Venetian architecture. Many streets have been pedestrianised and and in the square, also traffic-free, cafés and restaurants occupy much of the space with outdoor tables. The museum (open daily, except Tuesdays, until mid-afternoon) has finds from Mycaenae and Tiryns and exhibits from the Revolutionary period. There is also a popular art museum open daily, except Tuesdays, all day.

Coast Road to Epidavros

Asine; Tolon

The road southeast, from Nafplion goes first inland and then weaves back seawards, past the rocky promontory that holds the ruins of ancient Asine with its relics of many periods (from the Helladic through Mycaenean, Hellenistic, Roman and Venetian), to the seaside resort of Tolon (hotels, restaurants and camp sites) which has greatly out-grown its sheltered little beach. Those with cars, however, can go back to the fork just before Asine and continue more or less parallel with the coast, through the hamlets of Drepanon, Vivari, Kallithea, Candia and Irion. No longer the peaceful, undeveloped coast it once was, it nevertheless attracts fewer crowds than the older resorts.

Kranidion; Galátas

Near Irion the road snakes inland through the hills to join the main road to Kranídion, the chief market town of Eastern Argolis, and the peninsula's tip at Portoheli and Kostas (boats for Spetse, hydrofoils for Piraeus), both heavily built up with villas and hotels. Another road from Kranidion, to Ermióni (more intensive development) continues the loop round the peninsula as far as Galátas (boats for Poros). Galátas, surrounded by lemon groves, is almost part of Poros town which it faces across the narrow strait. Behind it, on the side of a hill, is the village of Dhamalá, or Trizína, and the few sparse remains of Theseus's capital of Troezen. The view from there is over the Methana peninsula, Poros, and the shoreline where the young Hippolytus, Theseus's son, accused of being the lover of his step-mother Phaedra, was devoured by a monster from the sea.

Methana; Ligourio

Methana, connected to Argolis by an isthmus so narrow that it is almost an island, is a pleasant uncommercialised little spa at the neck of promontory, with sulphur springs nearby. Hydrofoils operate to and from Piraeus. The mainland road continues along the coast for a few miles past the turn-off to Methana, and then turns inland to complete the circle not far from the crossroads-village of Ligourio, with two or three pretty little Byzantine churches and a couple of *kaffeneions*. From here Epídavros (Epidauros) is a matter of 15 kilometres (10 miles) away.

Epídavros

The highlight of Epídavros is of course the huge Classical theatre, with its fantastic acoustics, where the annual festival is held; it has been restored for this purpose but is basically of the 4th century BC. In ancient times this was only part of a combined spa-cum-sanctuary with temples, baths, accommodation, a gymnasium and a stadium. Their ruins are scattered but, especially in the winter and early spring when carpets of flowers bloom beneath the trees, it is pleasant to stroll among them. The site is open daily all day; the museum (closed on Tuesdays) has interesting model reconstructions of the complex and some minor finds from the site. The major ones are in Athens. The attractive and lively seaside village of Old Epídavros is a possibility for lunch; for a quiet swim New (Nea) Epídavros is far less built up.

The Argo-Saronikos Islands

The Argolis peninsula is fringed with islands, of which the four important ones are Aegina (pronounced Egg-eena), Poros, Hydra (pronounced Eedhra) and Spetse. All are connected by boat and hydrofoil with Piraeus and one can end a bus tour of Argolis by crossing to Spetse and thence island-hopping back to the capital.

Spetse

Spetse, the smallest (pop. c. 3,500) and for generations the most socially chic of the four, is relatively green, especially with olive groves; its beaches and beauty spots must be reached either on foot, by boat, horse-drawn cab, bicycle or scooter, as cars are restricted. Its town (several hotels) is gay and charming, ranged round a historic little square by the jetty where its defence cannon were mounted; several remain as decorations. A picturesque old harbour full of boatyards lies to the east, protected by a chapel.

Hydra

Hydra (pop. c. 2,500), long, narrow, spiny and forbiddingly barren, and also car-less, has a long and imposing seafaring tradition and has given birth to many a Greek naval hero. Its town, full of the 18th century mansions of wealthy maritime families, rises in a sheer multi-coloured amphitheatre round the deep harbour: streets are mostly flights of cobbled stairs and steep lanes. Churches to see include the Mitropoleous, Aghios Ioannis, and the monasteries above the town; Aghia Triáda and Zourvas monasteries along the coast, like the (poor) beaches, are best reached by small boats plying from the main quayside. Popular, like its sister islands, with Athenians at weekends as well as with more sophisticated tourists, it has half a dozen hotels and pensions, plenty of restaurants and *kaffeneions*, and a night life that tends to be more plentiful and noisier, particularly along the quay, than in most Greek islands.

Poros

Poros (pop. c. 4,000), separated by a narrow channel from the mainland, is strictly only the name of the principal town (built on its own little limestone peninsula) of the island of Kalavria, but the whole island is usually called by that name. The town itself, predominantly blue and white, is piled above the quay with numerous *tavernas* and *kaffeneions*, inns and hotels; more hotels lie on the outskirts and it is all very lively and popular. East of the town the Monastery of Zoodokhos Pighí sits on a pine-covered slope above a pleasant beach; inland of it, in a saddle between two hill-tops, is a ruined Sanctuary and Temple of Poseidon, with a lovely view. Pine-fringed beaches stretch away to the west of the town.

Aegina

Aegina (pop c. 6,000), sloping away in nut, fruit and olive groves from the almost symmetric cone of mountain at its southern apex, is historically the most important of the four islands, due to its strategic position in the middle of the Saronic Gulf. It was occupied long before Mycaenean times by worshippers of the mother-goddess Aphaia; it became wealthy in Archaic and Classical times through shipping, pottery and bronze-founding. It earned the displeasure of Athens by sporadically supporting its enemies (although it fought with Athens against the Persians at Salamis) and was eventually defeated and depopulated by Athens in the 4th century BC. In later history it was a Venetian stronghold. Its chief town, which has several small inns and three grander hotels, two of them well out of town, is on the site of the ancient one in the northwest. Flattish and at first sight uninteresting, it has some mediaeval and earlier remains, and a small museum (open daily until mid-afternoon except on Tuesdays) that houses, among other things, an Attic sphinx figure, examples of the local ancient coinage, imprinted with a turtle, and local pottery. Buses run regularly to pretty, lively Aghia Marina (hotels, tavernas) in the north-east, passing the 13th century Omorfi Eklesia church with its fine frescoes, and the ghost town of Paleiochora, once the island capital, and miles of pistachio plantations. Above Aghia Marina is the important and lovely Archaic Temple of Aphaia (open daily until mid-afternoon), its grey limestone Doric columns rising above the pines and commanding wonderful views of the Attic coast.

Southern Peloponnese
Gulf of Argolis

Back again at Argos, the main southern Peloponnese road runs through citrus and other fruit groves. Just 5 kilometres (3 miles) from the town is a signpost (right) to Kefallári where a river runs out of a cave and café tables are set out beneath the planes and poplars. The ancients believed the waters came underground from Lake Stymphalía, entrance to the Underworld, and the spot was sacred to Pan and Dionysos. At the village of Myloi on the Gulf of Argolis, several roadside booths sell *souvlakia*, and there are *kaffeneions*. Just beyond it are the important Early Helladic excavations, small and well labelled, of Lerna, where legend has it that Herakles slew the many-headed Hydra.

Thereafter, a left-hand fork leads along an occasionally dramatic corniche road and some of the prettiest and least-developed coastal scenery in the Peloponnese with scores of empty coves and fine pebble beaches between green and hilly headlands. Paralion Astros, with hotels edging the semi-sandy beach and another on the harbour, trails down a hill crowned with a Frankish castle; Astros, the big prosperous village inland of it, has the charming Loukou Monastery and Byzantine church behind it; Aghios Andreas inland, has a small beachside sibling alongside an unexcavated citadel; Tiros is substantially built up but Krionéri, a bay with a fresh water spring bubbling up through its beach, is still quite undeveloped.

Leonidhion
Leonídhion, at the end of this coast road, is a delightful huddle of old houses and shady squares at the edge of a fertile small plain noted for its succulent early fruit and vegetables.

Parnon Mountains
A fine new road, smooth-surfaced for all but about eight of its 48 kilometres length (five out of 30 miles, and even the rougher parts are hard-packed) now leads south from Leonidhion, making for an infinitely prettier route between Argos and Sparta, or Monemvasia, than the inland main road. To begin with it follows a series of dramatic gorges through the Parnon mountains, above the course of a river, with stunning glimpses of the whitewashed monastery of Elona tucked into the top of a copper-hued cliff face. The plateau beyond is remote and empty but for colonies of bee-hives, flocks of goats, and the solitary slate-roofed village of Kosmas, beyond which is a monument to 1943 resistance fighters,

Geraki
The hill-village of Geraki (pronounced Yeraki) proclaims itself as "Byzantine", shamelessly assuming the mantle of the castle beyond; nevertheless it is pretty enough and has at least one good *taverna* with splendid views. The castle, and town that supported it, lie up a steep hillside, reached by a rough track that turns off the road just past a pretty Byzantine church and cemetery. It was built in imitation of Mistras (see below) by a Frankish baron, Jean de Nivelet, in 1254, and taken from him barely 40 years later by the Byzantines. It is a good introduction to Mistras and without the crowds; a succession of ruined houses and chapels, some with interesting carvings and frescoes (the guardian, when he makes his appearance, will unlock the better-preserved ones, and expects a tip). At the summit, the castle precincts are extensive but ruinous and there is another church. The

views from its shady terrace are stupendous.

Arcadia; Sparta; Monemvasia

The main (inland), road, taking the right fork after Lerna, signposted to Trípolis, climbs in hairpin bends up the steep Ktenias range, over the ridge and down into the wide, flat plateau of Trípolis, the heart of Arcadia, mountainous, bare and rugged — not at all the leafy pastoral scene of Poussin's imagination. Capital of the modern *nome* of Arkadias, Trípolis is a busy industrial town (pop. c. 22,000), unlovely but with some excellent restaurants and a couple of hotels. North of it lie the remains of two once-great Peloponnesian cities, Mantinea and Orchomenos. Not to be confused with the Orchomenos in Boeotia, this city, with traces of the great walls that once surrounded it, has a gentle, melancholic atmosphere perhaps because the great Theban general, Epanimondas, met his death here.

Sparta

Continuing south the road passes the uninspiring site of ancient Tegea, squeezes through a mountain pass, and then crosses the Evrotas river to Sparta (pop. c. 12,000), at the foot of the Taygetos range. The remains of the ancient city-state whose pre-eminence was in the field of battle and whose upbringing of the young was so cruelly severe, slumber among the olive and fruit groves to the north of the town, not far from the road. They convey nothing of the might of the ancient city, so feared that defence walls were unnecessary and so dedicated to war that artistic achievement was scorned. There is a theatre beside the ruins of a 10th century basilica and a few stones marking the sites of a sanctuary, an altar and a temple. Modern Sparta, a low-built town with wide streets and a good many hotels, houses the museum (open daily, except Tuesdays, until mid-afternoon); it contains some stern Laconian sculpture. More cheerful are the Roman mosaics from a later age, a few minutes' walk away.

Mistras

It is almost a relief, however, to shrug off the grim associations of ancient Sparta and go on to Mistras, a few miles away. The Frankish adventurers, who originally founded the fortress there after the Fourth Crusade sacked Constantinople, were also warlike but their successors were Byzantine despots (Governors) who enriched the mediaeval town with churches and palaces. The ruins, on a steep hill fragrant with the scent of herbs and increasingly peaceful as you toil upwards (coach tours do not as a rule stop long enough for more than a cursory visit to the lower town) contain some of the loveliest 14th and 15th century frescoes in Greece. Especially noteworthy are those in the Cathedral of Aghios Dimitrios (where the last Byzantine Emperor was crowned); the Pantanássa, now occupied by nuns, with a lovely view from its terrace; Aghioi Theodori and the Panaghia Hodigitria, both in the Vrontokhion monastery complex; and the Perivleptos. The Palace of the Despots, various houses, and the remains of Geoffrey de Villehardouin's original Frankish castle, at the summit, are all worth the effort it takes to reach them. Half a day is not too long to allow for the visit; the site is open every day, all day; the museum, in the Bishops' Palace, closes mid-afternoon and all day Tuesdays.

Monemvasia
South of Sparta, on the easternmost of the three fingerlike peninsulas that fringe the southern Peloponnese, is another Frankish Byzantine stronghold, later captured by Venice. Monemvasia (pop. c. 650), clinging to the seaward side of a cone of rock not unlike Gibraltar, linked to the mainland (village, hotels and beach) by a long causeway, is one of those unexpectedly romantic places that make exploring Greece such a joy. On the other side of its gigantic bastioned gateway, an enchanting network of narrow cobbled alleys covers the hillside, running beneath arches and between noble, sometimes crumbling mansions — though many have been expensively restored — and past numerous churches. Below is the sea; above are the huge fortifications of the *kastro* and, within them, perched on a dizzying cliff edge, the glorious Byzantine church of Aghia Sophia. Once famous for its Malmsey wine, Monemvasia was half-forgotten for years until romantically-minded conservationists turned their attentions upon it. Even now, although there are a few cafés and souvenir shops, the only serious eating place is Maroula's *taverna* and there are very few rooms for rent. Late at night, when the day visitors have left, it must feel desolate; perhaps fortunately, the mainland village (Yefíra) is anything but. The only other sizeable town on this peninsula is the little port of Neapolis on the southern-most bay, best reached by sea (boats from Nafplion ply up and down the coast as far as Kithira) but also accessible by road.

Mani
The central finger of the Peloponnese is the mountainous and little-visited Mani, extolled by Patrick Leigh Fermor in his book of that name; it ends in the seaman's much-dreaded Cape Matapan. Gytheion, its capital (connected to the islet of ancient Cranae, where Paris and Helen paused in their flight from Sparta to Troy), is a peaceable, charming, colour-washed little port (pop. c. 3,400) with a few smallish waterfront hotels that book up quickly at weekends; there are others to the south of the town. There are *tavernas* in the square at the southern end of the inner harbour and many more, specialising in fish, round the corner along the outer harbour. Hundreds of British troops were evacuated from Gytheion, with the villagers' help, during World War II, an episode remembered with pride by its older inhabitants. The road across the northern part of the Mani affords fine views of its dramatically wild, craggy scenery, with sentinel watch-towers built by warring Maniot families standing against the skyline. Areopolis, gateway to the Deep Mani, is a large, white and sunny

market village with a couple of intriguing, primitively-decorated churches; just south of it, on the coast, are the twin villages of Pyrgos and Diros, principally visited for their spectacular sea caves.

The Deep Mani
Continuing south, the country gets more barren and remote and the towers, so far seen singly, become profuse, apparently topping every hill and each clustered about with smaller stone-built houses; some of these "villages" are so close together that the belligerent Maniots could almost have fired on their quarrelsome neighbours without leaving their beds. Most of the towers had their upper storeys demolished when efforts were being made by the Turks to pacify the Mani; some are being restored as private houses (the National Tourist Office plans to take some over to convert into "traditional settlements" for tourists to rent, but so far has only completed one tower, near Areopolis). Others are near-ruinous, abandoned by their owners when freedom dawned and it was safe to leave their fortified homes and seek a living elsewhere. The landscape, wild as it is, is lovely, spiked with cypresses and peppered with small churches; it lends itself to exploration on foot.

Coastal villages
Geroliménas (pronounced Yerolimenas, pop. c. 70), is a tiny, simple and picturesque fishing port with two basic inns and a handful of *kaffeneions* and *tavernas*; beyond it, Vathia is a fair-sized and immensely evocative tower-village, almost deserted (pop. c. 40), and with no tourist facilities. South of that is Porto Kaghio and Cape Matapan (Akri Tenaro). A road follows the opposite, east, coast of the Mani back to Areopolis then continues to hug the west coast northwards towards Kalamata. It passes through a succession of attractive seaside villages, some with towers, some with small Byzantine churches, some with hotels: Itilou, Aghios Nikonas, Langada, Nomitsi, Aghios Nikolaos, Stoupa. At Thalame the so-called "Mani Museum" is well worth missing; Kardamili (pop. c. 300), on the other hand, just before the road leaves the sea for its final approach to Kalamata, is well worth a stop. Largest and prettiest of the Outer Mani resorts, it has been developed with reticence and has a fine pebble beach, numerous good *tavernas* and a handful of hotels and *pensions*.

South-west Peloponnese
Kalamata and Messinía
If you bypass the Mani, the direct route from Sparta to the south-western Peloponnese is across the magnificent Taygetos mountains to Kalamata (pop. c. 42,000) capital of richly fertile Messinia. A busy modern industrial town and port, famous for its olives, and oil, it was badly damaged by an earthquake in 1986 and much reconstruction needs to be done. Its only monument is a (Frankish) Villehardouin

castle. Beyond it, watered by the Pamisos River, is the beautiful Messinian plain, thick with fruit groves (even dates and bananas grow here), cotton and wheat fields; in antiquity fiercely coveted by Sparta, who waged punitive wars against the Messinians for its possession. To the north rises Mount Ithome, to whose summit the Messinians were forced to retreat. There are no ruins, but an abandoned convent, from which the view is stupendous. On a lower foothill, however, past the little village of Mavromati, is the remains of the Arcadian Gate: entrance to the colossal fortifications of ancient Messini. The walls, designed to enclose the city's farmlands too, are nearly six miles long and wind through fig and olive groves; the ruins of the city itself, which include a tiny theatre and an Askleipeion (signposted ΑΡΧΑΙΟΛΟΓΙΚΟ ΧΟΡΙΟ), open daily until mid-afternoon, are on the opposite edge of the site and are still being excavated.

Koroni and Methoni
South again, past busy modern Messini (airport), a left fork runs down the coast to the pretty village of Koroni (pop. c. 1,400, with *tavernas* and a few small hotels — one on a magnificent beach south of the town — and *kaffeneions*) spilling down from a splendid Venetian castle to a picturesque harbour. Within the castle walls, partly made of older Classical stones, is a convent.

A perfectly passable road winds through the vineyards and the olive groves and past beaches at the promontory's tip to Methoni (pop. c. 1,300). Its magnificent Venetian fortress (open daily, all day) lapped by the sea, opposite the island of Sapientsa, is one of the most impressive in all Greece and the detour to this remote corner of the Peloponnese is worthwhile for the castle alone. Nothing remains of the Mycaenean city which originally stood here but the Venetian ruins and the tiny Turkish islet-fort beyond them are wonderfully evocative. Behind them is an immense sandy beach with the gradually-growing village at its edge. Beside an untidy open space that could become an attractive *plateia* if taken properly in hand are a couple of hotels, an inn and a *taverna* and *kaffeneion* or two; little else disturbs the peace.

Bay of Navarino
A good road runs for 12 kilometres (7½ miles) up the coast from Methoni to Pylos (pop. c. 2,500), on the southern tip of the huge Bay of Navarino where Greece's allies, headed by a British fleet under the command of Admiral Lord Codrington, inadvertently destroyed the Turkish fleet in 1827. (The intention had been merely to convince the Ottomans of the Allies' commitment to the Greek cause, but in that confined space engagements were inevitable and in under four hours the Sultan's fleet had been decimated. The Sultan subsequently negotiated). Skeletal remains of Turkish ships can sometimes be seen (on early mornings when the water is calm) at the bottom of the bay, close to the shore of Sphacteria Island, which almost shuts the

mouth of the bay off from the sea. A boat trip round the bay is recommended, to see the various Navarino memorials and also the plateau of Sphacteria, where the Spartans were badly defeated by the Athenians in 425 BC during the Peloponnesian War. The ancient city of Pylos was above the northern end of the bay where a mole still exists. From it, a path winds steeply up to the Venetian-fortified acropolis of Old Pylos (no remains); on its other (northern) flank is a huge cave, "Nestor's Cave", said to have stabled Neleus's and Nestor's oxen and also to be that in which the baby Hermes hid Apollo's sacred cattle. Below this is an almost circular shallow bay of fine sand where the boatman will wait while one swims.

Modern Pylos is an elegant town of creamy, well-proportioned houses and colonnades around three sides of an immense plane-shaded *plateia* the fourth side of which gives on to the sea. Numerous *tavernas* and *kaffeneions* in the *plateia*; around it, and on the waterfront leading away from it towards the vast Turkish fort that overlooks the town, are several hotels. There is a small museum (open daily, except Tuesdays, until mid-afternoon) and a new underwater archaeology centre, converted from a former jail, where finds are studied and restored for display.

Palace of Nestor
The important Myceanean Palace of Nestor (open daily until mid-afternoon) is some 10 miles north of modern Pylos, near the village of Hora (with another small museum; same opening hours, displaying frescoes and other palace finds). The site is particularly interesting because — although no surrounding city or fortifying walls exist — the palace itself is more complete than any of its contemporaries (even a bathtub remains) and gives the clearest idea of a Bronze Age palace layout.

Northwards the road follows the western Peloponnese coast — mostly dullish, but with a few leavening features. First is Filiatrá, where you cannot miss seeing a small-scale replica of the Eiffel Tower in the main street. It was one of the gifts of a village son who became a successful physician in the USA and returned to endow his home town with this and other follies — plus a library. Further on is his "medieval castle" and a horse-shaped summer house by the sea. Further north still, Kiparissia is a modern town (pop. c. 4,000) dominated by a Frankish castle; beyond it, some Mycaenean royal tombs have been excavated.

Central Peloponnese

Inland to Megalopolis
After crossing the river Nedas, and some 18 kilometres (11 miles)

before Pirgos, a side road to the right winds inland through beautiful hills to the charming old village of Andritsena (pop. c. 850), a muddle of crooked wooden houses balanced on a mountain ledge, its main square shaded by a gigantic plane tree. It has two attractive churches, one hotel, two inns and a couple of *tavernas*.

Bassae

Andritsena is the jumping-off place for one of the loneliest and loveliest of Classical temples: that of Apollo Epikourios, or Bassae, open daily until mid-afternoon, but under restoration. It was built by one of the architects of the Parthenon, Ictinos, and was one of the earliest temples to have an internal frieze (now in the British Museum, London). Its tall, greyish Doric columns, surrounded by open hillsides that are flower-covered in spring, are impressively majestic in their isolation. Beyond it, twisting down to Megalopolis, there is a fantastic view across the Alpheios valley of the great Frankish fortress of Karitaina, towering over the picturesque mediaeval village that straggles away from it along a ridge; it has several attractive old churches, notably that of Aghios Nikolaos. Below Karitena the road forks, the northerly "prong" twisting up to Dimitsána and Vytina (see below). The southbound turn off leads to the main Tripolis-Kalamata road (eventually to become the "old" road when the new highway is built) at Megalopolis.

Megalopolis

The scattered fragmentary remains of the ancient city of Megalopolis (founded, like Messini and Mantinea, by Epanimondas of Thebes as bastions against the might of Sparta) lie outside modern Megalopolis (pop. c. 5,000) close to the junction with the main road and a huge power-plant complex, mercifully invisible from the ancient theatre, though not from other parts of the site. Above it are the lonely ruins of Lykósoura.

Pirgos; Olympia to Dimitsána

The west coast road continues from the Andritsena turnoff to Pirgos in Elis, a large dull inland market and currant-producing town. Its port, where cruise ships call, is Katákolo, on the landward side of a small peninsula; Aghios Andréas, on the seaward side, has a good beach. A good road follows the fruitful Alpheios valley inland from Pirgos; there is also a short-cut just north of Kaiáfas (hot springs feed a thermal lake), via Krestena, that cuts out Pirgos altogether if you come from the south. Another narrow but good (and pretty) road winds down to Krestena from Andritsena.

Olympia

Olympia, in an unexpectedly green and leafy hollow, is at first a dis-

The Peloponnese and Argo-Saronikos

appointment: the village, with its many hotels and tourist shops, hides the ruins of the great sanctuary to which ancient Greeks of all ranks and styles from all over the country flocked every four years for over a millennium to celebrate the Games festivities. And the sanctuary itself, razed in 426 by order of the Christian emperor and later shaken by earth tremors, is a tangle of fallen columns, walls and masonry strewn beneath trees beside the Kladeos, a tributary of the Alpheios. Open daily all day (shorter hours for the museum on Tuesdays), the sanctuary is a complicated group of athletic quadrangles, stadium-temples, altars, treasuries, offices and officials' dwellings. They are often difficult to decipher even with a guide but the setting, particularly in the early morning or evening, is magical and it is deeply satisfying to wander, sit and gently contemplate, until the ancient scene seems to come to life of its own accord.

Olympia Museum

The new museum at Olympia, across the road from the site but included on the same admission ticket, is impeccably laid out; if you go round it clockwise, you start at the Myceanean period and end with the Roman. In the central hall are tactful reconstructions of the pediments of the Temple of Zeus. It is immensely rich, comparable with the best in the country: highlights include beautiful Myceanean and Archaic bronze horses, heads, pots, armour, and small figurines; the delightful coloured terracotta group of Zeus abducting Ganymede, and a fine terracotta warrior's horse; votive helmets left by overseas competitors in the games, including one each from Persia and Etruria; some skilfully carved Classical and Hellenistic marble statues, including the famous Hermes of Praxiteles.

Dimitsána and Langadia

Tourists speeding between Olympia and Athens go along the south coast of the Gulf of Corinth; another route is through Tripolis, va Karkalou, and the surprisingly Alpine-looking village of Vityna with its surrounding pinewoods. It has three inns and an Xenia motel; visitors come to walk in the summer and to enjoy snowy scenes in winter. A side road from Karkalou, eventually leading back to Andritsena, brings you to the mediaeval hill village of Dimitsána, birthplace of Bishop Germanos of Patras, proclaimer of the War of Independence. It is a charming place, protected from development, with a small hotel. Below it is the 12th century monastery of Aghios Ioannis Prodromos, and at Ipsounda, a lovely village slightly further along, are two attractive little late-Byzantine churches. The Karkalou-Olympia road winds on up through Langadia, a big village now very tourist-orientated since buses stop for people to admire the view, passes the turn-off for Tropea, another delightful village en route to the huge Ladon dam, and continues more gently down into the Ladon and Alpheios valleys.

Northern Peloponnese

Pirgos to Dhiakoftó

Continuing along the coast, north from Pirgos, the flat main road runs slightly inland; to the west are small seaside villages and a big tourist hotel near the Skafidhia Monastery. Inland of it is Amalias, a sizeable modern town. At Gastouni a road goes left for Loutra Killini (spa, hotels, sandy beach) and another goes right, inland, to the site of Ancient Elis, where Herakles cleaned the Augean Stables.

Elis; Pineios Dam

New excavations have not turned up anything startling in the way of ruins; certainly no discernible stables, but there is a small, grassy theatre and a modest museum (open daily, except Tuesdays, until mid-afternoon) with a handful of interesting objects notably a beautiful bronze *hydria*, or water vessel. Beyond it is the huge Pineios Dam, and by following a poorish track eastwards for about eight kilometres (five miles) you come to the dramatically perched village of Aghia Triáda and an excellent road, through ravishing country, that takes you north to Patras.

The alternative is to return to the main road, cross the Pineios and go through Andravidha, after which there is another turning west for Killini, once Glarentza, the ancient port of Elis (ferry boats for Zakinthos). South of it, near the village of Kastro, is the vast bulk of the strikingly well-preserved hexagonal Frankish Castle of Hlemoutsi, also called Castel Tornese by the Venetians. It is open daily until mid-afternoon. Between it and Patras the country is flat, thickly planted with fruit and vineyards, with one sizeable village (cheerful Kato Achaia) and a few accessible beaches.

Patras

Patras (pop. c. 142,000) is a lively port town (steamers for the Ionian islands and Italy and also for Athens via the Corinth Canal) with plenty of hotels and restaurants, wide streets, some arcaded, laid out on the grid system. Byron first set foot in Greece here, and it is also the birthplace of the Greek national poet, Palamas. Its pre-Lenten carnival is particularly colourful. It has a big new cathedral enshrining the head of its patron, Saint Andrew, who originally converted the citizens to Christianity; other holy relics of the saint were stolen by the Byzantines and yet others were taken to Scotland by the Bishop of Patras (St Regulus) who founded St Andrew's in Fife. There is also a Roman theatre (Odío) and, above it, an Acropolis that has been fortified since earliest times: traces of nearly all periods can be seen, and the view across the Gulf is marvellous.

Rio; Eghion

Five miles north-east of Patras is Rio, watched over by the sombre

The Peloponnese and Argo-Saronikos

Castle of the Morea, facing the Castle of Roumeli at Antirio on the northern shore; both are Turkish, built on more ancient foundations. From Rio a new highway parallels the old road along the Corinthian Gulf coast, which links a string of pine-shaded resort-villages (beaches mostly of fine pebbles) backed by vineyards rising into the mountain foothills. Eghion is another little port town (car ferries across the Gulf to Itea, the port for Delphi); just east of it, by the village of Rizomilos, is the presumed site of ancient Heliki, submerged by a tidal wave in the 4th century BC.

Megaspileion Monastery; Kalavrita

At Dhiakoftó a toylike railway crawls up the Vouraikos Gorge as far as Kalavríta, a unique, not to say senstational, experience. (There is also a good road). The train stops at Zakhlorou (inn and restaurant), from which a steepish path zigzags up to the Megaspíleion Monastery, rebuilt rather dully after an explosion in 1934 and also reachable by car. In its treasury, among other ikons, is the miraculous blackish wax-etched Ikon of the Panaghia (Virgin Mary) discovered in a cave by St Euphrosyne and two monks, and supposedly executed by St Luke. Also accessible by road from Patras and (a beautiful drive through high, fertile valleys) from Tripolis, Kalavríta (pop. c. 1,800) is a cool mountain resort doubly important to Greeks. The revolt against the Turks in 1821 started when Bishop Germano of Patras officially raised the revolutionary standard at the Monastery of Aghia Lavra (small museum) above it. In 1943 the entire male population was slain by the Germans in reprisal for guerilla activity: the hour of the massacre (2.34) is still shown on the Cathedral clock.

Dhiakoftó to Sikion

East of Dhiakoftó the Gulf becomes wider and there are stupendous views, changing hourly with the light, of Parnassus on the northern side and the Acro-Corinth at its head. The resorts continue, the biggest being Xylókastro, but you miss them all if, instead of taking the old coast road, you use the faster National Road just inland of it. It is in either case essential not to speed through or past Kiatro, from where a small branch road leads to one of the prettiest small sites in the Peloponnese, ancient Sikion (open daily until mid-afternoon). It was one of the oldest cities on the Peloponnese as well as one of the most artistic, but the lone slender column that rises from a cornfield to mark the site of the Doric gymnasium, with its lovely fountain and the theatre behind it, date from Hellenistic times. Below them (the only building in sight) is a Roman bath converted into a museum (temporarily closed at the time of writing) containing some fine Roman mosaics. The setting is ravishing.

Stymphalia; Kastánea; Nemea

Another road from Kiato climbs the rugged slopes of Kyllíni, drops behind it, and arrives at the marshy shores of the Stymphalia Lake, traditional gateway to the Underworld, where Herakles slew the

Stymphalian birds. A temple of Artemis and a 13th-century basilica, both ruined, stand on its shores, and the walled acropolis of the ancient city sits on a hilltop at the lake's western end, giving fantastic views of the lonely plain. Below the acropolis, a road leads to Kastánea, a summer mountain resort. The waters of the lake flow eastward, underground, and emerge in bubbling springs at Kefallari, a shady spot with *tavernas* along the Gulf of Argolis. From the eastern end of the lake it is also possible to reach Nemea, along a very passable and beautiful road that forks at Psari (*tavernas*); one arm connects with the main Corinth-Argos road after Nemea; the other, equally attractive, snakes southwards to join the Tripolis-Olympia road.

Meteora Monastery

Central Greece, Evia and the Sporades

Central Greece: Boeotia

Boeotia

The way to Central Greece from Athens lies through Boeotia, a curiously colourless region despite its trio of important Mycaenean cities — Gla, Orchomenos and Thebes — and its battlefields — Leuctra, Platea and Chaironeia — and its famous sons — Pindar, Plutarch and Hesiod. In Classical times its power was confined to the brief period of Theban supremacy under Epanimondas. It constitutes the neck of land between Attica and the rest of mainland Greece, traversed by two roads: the National Road to the north, which parallels the coast most of the way, and the old road through Thebes and Levadhia to Delphi. One visits its sights in passing rather than making a goal of them: which is by no means to denigrate their interest to the true Grecophile.

Through Thebes to Orchomenos

The old road to Thebes branches northwards just after Elefsis, passes the turn-off to Egósthena beneath the fortified hillock called Eleutherai, and descends to the village of Erithrai. Beyond it are the widespread remains of ancient Pleteá, at one time a staunch ally of Athens and razed by the Spartans, after a long siege, in 427 BC. Just before Thebes another left turn leads to Leuktra, marked by its marble Tropaion memorial, where in 371 BC Epanimondas defeated the Spartans.

Thebes

Thebes itself is disappointingly modern: the city legendarily founded in the 14th century BC by the Phoenician, Cadmus, brother of Europa and the sower of the dragons' teeth; the city of Dionysos and of Oedipus's parents, Laius and Jocasta, lies beneath the grid-like streets covering the acropolis of the present-day town. But the museum (open daily, except Tuesdays, until mid-afternoon) has some good archaic scupltures and funerary reliefs, pottery, seals, mosaics and Tanagra terracotta figurines.

Beyond Thebes, a lonely side road leads past the few remains of ancient Thespiai and the bigger ones of ancient Thisbe, to the south of the village of Dhomvrena. Here the road forks, the left-hand one leading eventually down to the Gulf coast and the other, very poor, snaking up the foothills of Mount Helikon to the Valley of the Muses. The last part is only passable on foot among the scattered ruins of the buildings associated with the four-yearly Mouseion festivals.

Fortress of Gla

North of Thebes there is a link road to the National Road, which skirts the two Boeotian lakes of Helike and Paralimni, lying beneath Mount Ptoion and the ancient oracular sanctuary of Apollo at Ptóo. The great fortress of Gla, once an island, is just off the main road: the remains of an ancient palace within gargantuan walls bigger than those of Tiryns. Another road, left off the National Road further on, skirts the northern rim of Lake Copaïs, long since drained, which originally surrounded Gla, and completes the detour by returning to the old road via Orchomenos and Levadhia.

Orchomenos

Orchomenos, capital of the Minyans, was one of the richest of Mycaenean cities (Gla was its dependency) but it had lost its importance by Classical times and was finally sacked by Thebes in 364 BC. Its remains consist of an impressive "beehive" tomb ("Treasury of Minyas"), excavated by Schliemann, the discoverer of Mycaenae. There are also a Classical theatre and a steep, fortified citadel with traces of many civilisations from the Neolithic down to the Macedonian. A 9th century Byzantine chapel, the restored Koimisistis Theotokou, is the earliest domed cross-in-square church in Greece.

Levadhia to Delphi

Levadhia is an agreeable cotton producing town (pop. c. 17,000), largely rebuilt since the War of Independence, (several hotels and *tavernas*) culminating in a Frankish castle. Tourist buses to Delphi stop in the lower part of town while passengers refresh themselves with *souvlakia*. Few bother to wander further up the hill where a prominent tower once housed a clock presented by Lord Elgin — he of the Parthenon marbles. Elgin was attempting to find the site of the oracle of Trophonios (still unidentified), whose suppliants had to drink the spring waters that still today cascade beneath plane trees and past *tavernas*. One spring was Lethe (forgetfulness) and the other, Mnemosyne (memory); between them they caused the suppliant to forget his past and remember only the apparently fearsome experience of his consultation with the subterranean oracle.

North of Levadhia, on the Lamia road, marked by the huge ancient stone Lion, is Chaironeia, where Philip of Macedon routed the southern Greeks in 338 BC. Two hundred and fifty years later, the same battlefield witnessed the defeat of the Greek general, Mithridates, by the Romans under Sulla.

Osios Loukas

Between Levadhia and Delphi the scenery becomes increasingly grand, dominated by Mount Parnassos. It is usual to branch south off the road, at a meeting-place of ways where Oedipus is said to have unwittingly killed his father, through Dhístomo (scene of a Nazi massacre in 1944) to the important and beautiful Monastery of Osios Loukas (open daily until mid-afternoon). Founded in the 10th century, this complex of buildings and its radiant mosaics and frescos constitute one of the principal Byzantine sights in Greece; the situation is lovely, too.

Parnassos

The Delphi road winds on and up round Mt Parnassos, passing through the prettily terraced, well-watered village of Arákhova, festooned with the wool rugs woven there, and noted for its wine. From there, a road leads up to the Parnassos ski-slopes, popular with walkers in summer; the main road descends in great bends for the first, breathtaking view of Ancient Delphi.

Delphi

The modern village (pop. c. 2,500) consists of one main street packed with hotels, restaurants, banks and souvenir shops (and people). Once it was bigger and more scattered, but much of it had to be razed when the French started excavating the site in 1892.

The monuments of the great oracular site of Delphi, dedicated since prehistoric times to the Pythian Apollo, cover a huge area on the slopes of Parnassos with one of the most staggering views in all Greece, across the "sacred" plain of olives to the glittering blue Gulf of Corinth and beyond, to the Peloponnese. Games and festivals were held here and the site was enriched by temples and treasuries contributed by all the major cities of the ancient world. It is open daily, all day long: probably the best time to visit is from about 1600 when the day-tours have departed.

Below the road from Arakhova is the Marmaria, or Sanctuary of Athena Pronaia, with the remains of several ancient temples dominated by the exquisite little Rotunda (early 4th century BC); beyond this is a gymnasium. Above, across a sharp bend in the road, is the Castalian Spring, above which Apollo, according to legend, planted a laurel tree: the priestesses and pilgrims to Delphi alike cleansed themselves here.

Temple of Apollo
The Sacred Precinct, with the Sacred Way winding up between the ruins of various treasuries to the great platform of the Temple of Apollo, is above the spring and the road, and dates from the 6th century BC. The restored columns of the temple rise majestically to the sky; beneath its floor is the entrance to the oracular cavern. Here the priestess, or Pythia, would sit upon Apollo's sacred throne and go into a trance, aided by the smoke of smouldering laurel leaves. She would then utter her prophecy, whose ambivalent terms would be interpreted, possibly even more ambivalently, by the attendant priests, and delivered to the suppliant. It only takes a superficial reading of ancient Greek mythology to discover how often the Pythia's prophecies were misinterpreted.

Theatre and Stadium
For the best views of all, climb on upwards to the 4th century BC. Theatre and, above it, the stadium (where the summer festival performances are given). Looking across the entire site from this vantage point, you can sense the awe Delphi inspired in the pilgrims of antiquity.

Museum
The museum is close to the road at the edge of the town and open for the same hours as the site, except on Tuesdays, when it closes. It contains among other things some marvellous Archaic sculptures and friezes, finds from the various treasuries, small bronzes and, of course, the famous bronze Charioteer of 475 BC.

Itea to Nafpaktos
Below Delphi the road winds down to the plain and through olive groves to Itea (pop. c. 4,500; ferries to Eghion), a fast-growing port

and industrial centre, thanks to the nearby bauxite mines, and to the cruise ship business. A road from there skirts the little gulf to Galaxhidi, once a ship-building centre in the days of wooden ships. Many of its handsome mansions have been, or are being, sensitively restored by artistically-minded incomers and the little town (pop. c. 1,200), once forlorn, is taking on a new air of subdued sophistication. Along its narrow harbour the beautiful old houses now have *tavernas* and *kaffenions* on their ground floors; there are two very pleasant small pensions. Across the harbour in the pine woods is an ancient monolithic tomb; the church of the Metamorfósis has a lovely altar screen and there is a little maritime museum with some primitive ship paintings. Beyond it, the coast road goes west to Nafpaktos (see below) past growing tourist development.

Inland, the road curls beside the course of the Pleistos up to Amphissa on the wooded slopes above it, famous for its olives, and dominated by a Frankish castle. Two roads lead away from here, one to the western extremity of Central Greece, winding round mountain spurs and through pine woods and neatly cultivated small-holdings past the huge and beautiful Mornos and finally down to the pretty little Venetian harbour town of Nafpaktos (Lepanto, off which the Turks lost an important naval battle in 1571). It has several small hotels, *tavernas* and *kaffeneions* and a good long beach of smooth pebble: an agreeable place for an overnight halt.

Amphissa to Karpenisi

The other road from Amphissa climbs northwards over the dramatically steep pass of Brallos. Just below it a turn-off to the left winds between two mountains, one of them Mount Iti, at whose summit Herakles died on a funeral pyre, in torment from the poisoned shirt of Nessos. (See also under Evinos). Both this road and the less attractive main one come down to the alluvial plain at the mouth of the Sperchiós river and to Thermopylae.

Thermopylae

This was the site of the famous battle of 480 BC in which Leonidas and 300 Spartans were annihilated by the Persians, who had managed to get round to their rear and attack both flanks. The plain has silted up and is considerably wider now, robbing the scene of much of its drama. There is a modern memorial; a statue of Leonidas, with his heroic utterances carved around its base; it is on the seaward side of the National Road off which (in the Athens direction) are, first, the spa of Kammena Vourla (many hotels; waters beneficial for rheumatic and arthritic complaints) and the growing resorts of Aghios Konstantínos (ferries to Skiathos and Skopelos) and Arkítsa (ferries to Aedipsos in Northern Evia).

Lamia and Karpenísi
Lamia (pop. c. 42,000) lies at the northern edge of the Spercheios delta; one of the chief towns of Central Greece, it is modern, clean and dullish. Inland and west of it, a good road follows the Spercheios to the nice modern country town of Karpenísi whose cool climate, and that of the villages of Mikró and Megálo Horió in the valley below it, is much favoured by Greeks; likewise the little spa of Ipati which is reached by a side road en route.

Central Greece: Thessaly

Lamia to Tríkala
North and west of Lamia the "old" road to the north crosses the Othrys foothills via the Furka pass and descends via Dhomokos to the great Thessalian plain. At Nea Monastíri it forks, the left-hand road going through Kardítsa, an uninteresting market town (turn off here for the attractive hillside spa of Smokovo), and Tríkala.

Tríkala (pop. c. 45,000) is lively and not without interest: two enormous *plateias* face each other, joined by a bridge across the trout-filled river that divides it (*tavernas* and hotels). A ruined sanctuary of Asclepeios, the healing deity, reputedly a native son, is near the Byzantine fort north of the river. Narrow market streets, some fine old mansions and Byzantine churches, and a former mosque complete its register of "sights". It is typically central-Greek and would be a pleasant place to stay in but for heavy, noisy traffic. As it is, the modern but not unattractive tourist dormitory-village of Kalambaka (pop. c. 5,900), 22 kilometres (14 miles) away, is a preferable base for exploring the Meteora region.

Meteora
This extraordinary cluster of sharp eroded pinnacles of rock erupting menacingly from the valley, many with monasteries at their summits, is one of the oddest sights in Greece. The monastic community was originally started by hermits in the late 13th century; during the Turkish occupation refugees swelled their numbers, but they dwindled during the 19th century and the incumbents of the few remaining monasteries are now chiefly occupied showing round visitors. Many have been abandoned altogether, one or two shelter small, closed communities and cannot be visited. Those that can are four in number and open from 0800 or 0900 until midday, and again from 1500 to 1800. Their "closed" days are indicated below.

Meteora Monasteries
A roughly circular route from Kalambaka links them but walking is

also involved. In former times, the monks reached them by means of retractable ladders, or in rope nets that were winched aloft; now the nets and pulleys remain — for show, and for hoisting in supplies — but steps have been cut into the rock-faces, steep in many cases. Aghios Nikolaos is up 230 steps; at the summit are twin 16th-century churches smothered in remarkable frescoes by Theophanes the Cretan, including a fine Last Judgment. The road twists round high-perched Roussanou (closed) to arrive at Varlaam (closed on Fridays) where the 142 steps have numbers painted on them. Its layout, around a courtyard, resembles that of the others except that a neat kitchen garden graces the courtyard. There are more fine 16th and 17th-century frescoes in the church; a good carved 16th-century iconostasis and a small museum displaying icons, old gospels, chalices and vestments.

Great Meteoron; Aghios Stephanos

Beyond Varlaam, the Great Meteoron (closed Wednesdays) is the largest and most easily accessible of the Meteora monasteries; it dates from the 14th century and the frescoes in the apse and chancel of its Church of the Metamorphosis are contemporary with it. The rest of the church, and the Refectory (another fine museum), were built in the 16th century. Another closed monastery, Aghia Triada, looks down from its pinnacle at the road as it continues to the nunnery of Aghios Stephanos (closed Mondays, few steps to climb). Renovations currently in progress have temporarily closed the older of its two churches; the newer one is late 18th-century. The rich small museum contains 16th and 17th-century icons, crucifixes, illuminated manuscripts and beautiful embroidery.

Lárissa to Pelion

Lárissa

A good road runs across the Thessaly plain from Trikala to Lárissa (pop. c. 102,000), a busy, thriving town, capital of Thessaly, built around a huge central square. Between the square and the river Pineios are the remains of a Byzantine fort and a small classical temple; there is also a covered market and a little museum in a former mosque, but it is hardly a tourist centre. Nor do many tourists seek out the ruins of Krannon to the south, not far from the main road that connects it (via Farsala, where Caesar defeated Pompey in 48 BC) with Lamia. Krannon was a major Thessalian town in antiquity; the ruins (badly signposted) include an Asclepeion temple and two Mycaenean-type *tholos* tombs.

Lárissa and the Thessalian plain are shut off from the sea by Mount Ossa to the north-east and Mount Pelion to the south-east. The National Road from the south, after Thermopylae, skirts the Euboean and Pagasai gulfs, (turn off to Glifa for a car-ferry to Evia) and then loops inland of the two mountains.

Pagasai Gulf
The road to Volos branches off midway between Lamia and Lárissa and follows the almost landlocked Pagasai Gulf. En route are several interesting minor sites: Sesklo (ruins of a large Neolithic palace, remains from even earlier); Dhimini (remains of a somewhat later Neolithic settlement of about 4000 BC and also of some much later Mycaenean *tholos* tombs, linking the site with Homeric legends); the early Christian city of Phthiotic Thebes at Nea Anchialos; and Demetrias-Pagasai (one just inland and the other its ancient port: widespread partly-walled remains including a theatre, temples and a palace). All three are open until mid-afternoon; Sesklo closes on Thursdays and Dhimini on Fridays.

Volos
Volos itself (pop. c. 72,000) is named after the ancient Iolkos, Jason's city, whence the Argonauts sailed to find the Golden Fleece — though Pagasai (see above) is a more likely contender for the actual location. An agreeable port-town (boats and hydrofoils to Evia and the Sporades), Volos has numerous hotels, *tavernas* along the waterfront, and one of the best provincial museums in Greece. Principal exhibits are Neolithic remains from Demetrias, Pagasai, Sesklo, etc.; over 300 marvellous painted grave stelae of the Hellenistic period, and some superb Hellenistic gold jewellery.

Pelion
South and east of Volos, Mount Pelion runs into the sea in the comma-shaped hilly Magnesia peninsula, thick with oak and beech forest, fruit, nut and olive groves where the legendary Centaurs lived; Cheiron, their leader, reared both Jason and Achilles. The verdance of this peninsula is cherished by Greeks, and its villages of white-washed half-timbered houses with jutting upper storeys and balconies, and grey stone roofs, are unique to this area and very charming. So, too, are the low, hall-shaped churches, often with exterior galleries and tiny apsidial niches. Portariá has an exquisite main square with a fountain, shaded by a gigantic plane tree; Makrinítsa, huddled inside its former fortifications, has thread-narrow streets and two small, pretty churches; Zagorá is a cluster of four villages clinging to the wooded slopes with rustic 18th century churches; Tsangaráda is more scattered.

Be warned however: roads are narrow and can become jammed; not only with tourist traffic but, at harvest times, with local vehicles collecting apple, pear and plum crops from the many orchards, and transporting pot-grown gardenias and other flowering shrubs from the nurseries to city markets. Even narrower side-roads lead down to seaside hamlets on the Aegean shore; Horefto, Milopótamos, Aghios Ioannis, all with fine-pebble beaches, pellucid seas and a handful of small hotels, *tavernas* and *kaffeneions*. The Gulf side of the peninsula is flatter and less dramatic, with extensive olive groves, and more small resorts between them. There are hotels in the principal mountain villages, too, including Xenias at Portariá and Tsangarada; none is big and in high season they become well-booked in advance and the chance visitor would do better to stay in Volos. At Vizitsa some of the fine old houses have been restored by the National Tourist Organisation for letting to visitors; further south, other old houses are rented out privately.

Evia

Evia (pronounced Evvia; in Greek, spelt Euboia), Greece's second largest island, is separated by a long, narrowish channel from the mainland of Boeotía and Attica and virtually split down its length by wooded mountains which make its east coast precipitous, difficult of access except for one port, Kimi (ferry to Skyros) and consequently undeveloped. In antiquity its chief cities were Halkis (the present capital, pop. c. 45,000) and Erétia; for over 100 years, until 1470, it was a Venetian stronghold.

Halkis
Halkis is connected by a bridge to the mainland (Turkish fortress) across the Evripos strait, which was spanned as early as 411 BC. It is an agreeable modern port town with a former mosque and a fountain in its main square, a Byzantine basilica (Aghia Paraskevi) converted by the Crusaders into a cathedral, good hotels and a small museum of finds from Erétria.

Erétria and Southern Evia
South and east of Halkis the road parallels the sea, crossing the vine-planted Lelantion plain with its mediaeval towers to Erétria (ferry to Skala Oropou, on the mainland), its neighbourhood heavily developed for tourism. Its ruins, destroyed in 87 BC and never rebuilt, lie up a hill behind the town: fragments of a palace, temple, theatre, gymnasium, sanctuary; and, away to the east, a Macedonian tomb with thrones and funeral couches. More ruins lie within the town: a temple of Apollo, a fountain and the mosaic of an ancient bath. The site is open daily until mid-afternoon; the museum (same hours) is closed on Tuesdays. Further on, high above Alivári in a mountain saddle, are the ruins (5th century BC houses) of ancient Dystos; thence a scenically beautiful road leads on southward to Karistos (boats for Rafina), a pretty seaside village with several inns.

Northern Evia
North of Halkis the main road runs diagonally across the island

through wooded valleys to Cape Artemesion and its temple ruins on the north shore. A branch road goes down to picturesque Limni and Roviae (Rovié) on the west coast; a remote Byzantine monastery lies to the south of them. Beaches and small seaside villages string along the north and east coasts, with Istia on the edge of the plain behind. The road ends at the cheerful little spa resort of Aidhipsos (sulphur springs) where there are many hotels and a car ferry to Arkitsa.

The Sporades

The four main islands of the Sporades trail away eastward from Pelion and the northern tip of Evia. They are connected by hydrofoil and ferry services with Volos, Thessaloniki and one another; ferries to Skiathos and Skopelos also operate from Aghios Konstantinos, near Kammena Vourla, on the mainland. Skiros is most directly reached from Kymi on Evia.

Skiathos

Fashionable Skiathos (pop. c. 4,000), nearest to the mainland, shares Pelion's forested verdance and is also endowed with fine beaches: Akhladias, Platania and Koukounariés are all developed with good-class hotels, sophisticated villa complexes and *tavernas*. The only town, Skiathos, has excellent waterfront tavernas and a fairly lively night life. Fringing the lower tiers of a wooded natural amphitheatre on the south-east coast, its harbour is protected by a causeway running out to a pine-covered islet with a memorial to the novelist Moraitidis (1851-1929). This is the site of the ancient town, but for 300 years during the Turkish occupation (1538-1829) it was abandoned for an almost inaccessible rock peninsula in the north, known as Kastro. By land, this means a walk of over two hours, passing two monasteries en route; it can also be visited by boat from the capital. Its ruins include a Church of Christ, with frescoes, and the Byzantine Convent of the Annunciation, still inhabited by one or two monks.

Skopelos

Skopelos, separated from Skiathos by a wide channel, is larger (pop. c. 4,500) and more cultivated (vines, olives, fruit) than its neighbour but far less developed touristically. Its capital, Khora Skopelou (villas, apartments and hotels), clings to a windy north-facing hillside above its harbour and beach; dazzlingly white with over 100 churches, many of them with locally-executed 17th and 18th century ikons and screens. Grey slate roofs, patterned with white ridge tiles, alternate with the white domes and archways of the churches. On the edge of the harbour are the remains of a Classical temple. Across the island, 45 minutes by road (buses) is a sheltered south coast harbour used as an alternative to that of Khora Skopelou in bad weather; at the island's northern tip, facing Skiathos, are the twin villages of Glossa and

Loutraki. Below them are a couple of beach hotels, *tavernas* and apartments.

Alónissos

Alónissos, across a narrow channel due east of Skopelos, is a mass of wooded hills rising to the peak of Mount Kouvouli. Barely developed, its waters are inhabited by monk seals, until a few years ago severely threatened; now the inhabitants take pride in their protection. The island has a picturesque old inland capital, Khora, abandoned after an earthquake in 1965. Below it on the south coast Patiriti is the modern capital and, with Votsi and Marpounta, the main resort area (several simple hotels).

Skiros

Skiros, largest, most easterly and least tourist-orientated of the quartet, consists of two hilly extremities linked by a narrower flattish plain in the centre. Legend has it that Achilles was hidden here by his mother, Thetis, who dressed him in girl's clothing to keep him from the Trojan war; here, too, Theseus was murdered by Lykomedes.

Skiros Town

The capital, Skiros, lies inland of and above a sandy beach on the fertile northern half of the island. It has picturesque, white cubic houses with flat roofs grouped along narrow streets below a ruined *kastro* with a Venetian gate and a convent within its walls which once encircled the acropolis of the ancient city. Below, at the eastern end of the town, is a modern statue of Rupert Brooke (see below) and, nearby, the Faltaits folk-museum (open late afternoons, every day), housed in a fine old mansion. Skiros has rooms to let, and pensions, but no hotels. There are *tavernas* in town and on the outskirts.

A road leads from Skiros town across to the island's main port, Linaria (ferry to Kimi, connections with the other Sporades), hedged by a trio of islets on the west coast.

Southern Skiros

The southern half of the island is covered with scrub and crossed by a rough but passable road. At its tip, up a little valley from the port of Tris Boukés, also reached by boat from Linaria, is the grave of the English poet Rupert Brooke who died in April 1915 aboard a French hospital ship, anchored there en route for the Dardanelles.

Northern Skiros

Another road goes part-way round the northern half of the island (turn-offs to beaches) where a military air base also does duty as a civil airport.

The Ruins of Philippi

Northern Greece and the North Aegean

Northern Greece

Macedonia (Makedonia) and Thrace were only integrated politically with the rest of the country in the early 20th century and northern Greece, geographically a continuation of the central region, becomes increasingly Balkan in character as it extends northwards.

The towering Pindos mountains form a natural barrier between central and western Greece. Only one road, latterly greatly improved, traverses this immense range, running west from Kalambaka and Metsovo to Ioannina.

Metsovo
Metsovo (pop. c. 3,000) is a once-remote and picturesque mountain village now experiencing a rush of tourism, thanks to the good new road and the development of ski-slopes above it. It has grown greatly and although all new buildings must adhere to the traditional style,

its character has inevitably changed: Vlach shepherds in their ethnic garb are far outnumbered by those who now wear contemporary clothing, and by visitors. It boasts a handicrafts museum, shops selling local cheese and crafts, the house of the statesman Averoff, and many rustic-style hotels.

Lárissa to Thessaloníki: coastal route

Ambelakia

The main road from Lárissa skirts Mount Ossa and passes the turn-off to Ambelakia. Just a short way uphill, this village of 500 inhabitants is another world. Once it boasted 4,000 inhabitants and Greece's first co-operative, established in the 17th century by silk-weavers who had migrated there. It prospered hugely until Ali Pasha, the Turkish ruler, raised their taxes and the Napoleonic wars ruined their European trade. Today its 30-odd fine 18th century homes are preserved and one, the Schwartz house, with painted panelling, wood-mosaic ceilings and other unique features, is open to visitors.

Vale of Tempe

The main road then runs through the well-wooded Vale of Tempe, sacred to Apollo, where the river Peneios joins the sea, and hugs the coastal strip beneath the foothills of Mount Olympos. This stretch of coast was once expected to enjoy a huge tourist boom which never materialised; it accordingly has a number of very adequate hotels on good beaches with a lot of space between them, starting at Platamonas with its startlingly romantic 13th century castle.

Litohoro and Dion

A turn-off, inland, leads to Litohoro (pop. c. 6,000) with small hotels, from which climbers start the ascent of Mount Olympos, ancient home of the gods.

The next inland turn-off brings you to the huge, recently-excavated site of Dion (Dio, open every day, day-long; museum closed on Tuesdays). It was a sacred city to both Philip II and Alexander the Great and the Romans subsequently paved its streets and introduced a sophisticated water-system. Excavations are still going on but there is already much to see: Greek and Roman theatres, a Roman bath-house, latrines, a Christian basilica, a Sanctuary of Isis, a grid-pattern of streets off which some of the buildings still have mosaic floors (the best of these are covered over in winter). The museum, in the nearby village, displays well-arranged finds including some charming *stelea,* bronze votives, a gold wreath and other jewellery, and the statue of Isis from her sanctuary.

The main road to Thessaloníki passes the market town of Katerini and crosses the Aliakmon, Loudias and Axios rivers on the approach to Thessaloníki, Greece's second city.

Lárissa to Thessaloníki: inland route

A natural inland circuit between Lárissa and Thessaloníki takes in the principal sights of Western Macedonia. This can be reached from Lárissa via Elassón with its Byzantine bridge over the Elassonitikos ravine and the Panaghia Olimpiótissa monastery above. After Elassón, a pretty road branches back to Katerini and the coast, giving access to the Mount Olympos ski-fields. Servia, in the Aliakmon valley, has a Byzantine fortress and a ruined Aghios Theodoros monastery. Alternatively, there is a good road from Kalambaka and the Meteora over beautiful upland agricultural country to Grévena. Kozani (pop. c. 31,000) which has an airport, hotels and bus centre, is the chief town of the region and a centre of the mining industry (lignite). Its church of Aghios Nikolaos has a good iconostasis and frescoes; the Metamorfósis tou Sotiros church on the outskirts lies on one of the main roads to Yugoslavia. To the north and west is the Lake District of Greece, a circuit starting at Siátista, a small 18th century town (pop. c. 5,700) that was once a wine centre and is now more occupied with the fur trade.

Kastoriá

From Siátista a road crosses and recrosses the Aliakmon valley through truly pastoral scenery to Kastoriá (pop. c. 20,000), legendarily founded by Orestes and re-established by the Emperor Justinian on a steeply-ridged neck of land projecting into a lake where the locals fish from unusual rectangular wooden boats. The town has numerous 18th century mansions the upper storeys of which project on timber over narrow cobbled streets; sadly, many of these are being allowed to fall into ruin. The scores of fur shops (this is the centre of the trade) add to its interest: the particular skill of the furriers is piecing together scraps into whole garments without revealing the joins. For the best of their wares, however, you need to shop in Athens. Even more interesting are a number of small Byzantine churches, often with exterior frescoes: to visit them (most are kept locked), apply to the Tourist Office. Aghioi Anaryíoi Varlaam, Panaghia Koubelitissa, Aghioi Apolsteloi, Aghios Stefanos, Aghios Georghios are among the most important in the town; the two Moni Mavrótissa churches are about an hour's stroll along the tree-fringed lake shore. There are several hotels, including a Xenia, and good *tavernas* around the market at the landward end of the isthmus.

Prespa Lakes and Florina

The road north from Kastoriá climbs behind the lake, with lovely views. Until quite recently, a special pass was needed for this part of the country because of the proximity of Albania; now, relations between the two countries have improved and there is a frontier-post open; the turn-off, about 26 kilometres (15-16 miles) north of Kastoriá, is signposted. The road is being improved, too, and is metalled for most of the way to Florina; the country through which it passes is remote, mountainous and thickly wooded. A turn-off some nine kilometres (five miles) after the Albania one takes you westwards, again along a good road with fine views, to the beautiful Prespa Lakes: Little Prespa, wholly within Greece, and Great Prespa, shared with Albania and Yugoslavia. There is a scatter of tiny hamlets; views of both lakes from the spit of land between them; swimming in the cold, reed-edged waters. At Microlimin, on Little Prespa, a *taverna* specialises in deliciously-cooked trout, and the whole area is rich in bird life. Florina (pop. c. 12,500) is an unremarkable modern town with a few hotels and a developing ski-area above it.

Edhessa

Beyond Florina, the forests give way to wide uplands and the road skirts Lake Vegoritida before dropping down into the open, fertile Edhesseos valley and reaching Edhessa (pop. c. 16,000). Here the river separates into several channels and plummets over the sheer cliff edge on which the town sits: a delightfully unexpected phenomenon. The water and shade-trees give a gay air to the town which is predominantly modern although it has a pretty old church, Koimisis tis Panaghias, a graceful Byzantine bridge, and the ruins of a Hellenistic city.

Macedonian Tombs

After Edhessa, turn south through Lefkadhia for the fantastic 3rd century BC Macedonian Temple Tombs scattered about the area between Lefkadhia and Naoussa. They are well-signposted, and normally open daily until mid-afternoon. The "Great Tomb" is that of a general and has a painted relief of a battle along its facade, as well as frescoes; others are frescoed brilliantly inside; all are delicately proportioned with delightful architectural details.

Veria

Veria (Veroia, pop. c. 37,000), at first sight entirely modern, has in fact a long history and from the latest Turkish occupation period some curious tiny churches survive. Mostly of wood, they were built in hidden corners and alleyways to escape notice and are worth hunting for. There is also a small museum (open daily, except Tuesdays, until mid-afternoon) and remnants of the ancient city walls are visible in places.

Philip II's Tomb

Just outside Veria is the now world-famous site of Vergina where an unlooted royal tomb, almost certainly Philip of Macedon's, was discovered in 1977.

The signposts are modest, simply signalling "Macedonian Tomb", and the site is not much to look at either, with a low, grassed-over tumulus opposite a café, apparently in the middle of nowhere since the village is out of sight of it. But it is hard not to feel a sense of history on looking into Philip's tomb: here, 2,300 years ago, a king was interred about whom we actually know quite a lot. Huge marble doors, now lying on the ground, separated the inner and outer chambers and a marble throne has been left in the inner one. The tomb is quite plain, with four Ionic columns on the facade and no interior frescoes; Philip II was assassinated and had to be buried quickly. Another tomb in the tumulus, this one painted, was that of a boy — identified as the young son of Alexander the Great — and some of its exquisite treasures are in the Thessaloníki Archaeological Museum along with the finds from King Philip's tomb. Yet another tomb in the same tumulus, still being excavated, may be that of Philip's mother Euridice, and the tomb of still another noble lady, discovered close to it in 1988, has yielded a unique pair of silver-gilt sandal soles, among other finds.

Philip II's Palace; Theatre
On a small plateau above the tumulus are Hellenistic ruins excavated in the last century and long known as "Palatitsa" or "little palace". Now it is authoritatively assumed to have been the palace of Macedonia's kings at their capital city of Aigai, before Aigai was superseded by Pella, and therefore Philip of Macedon's palace. Although it was subsequently built over, it is still possible to trace the palace outlines, and there are mosaics still in place. Below this, on a gentle slope, Professor Manolis Andronikos, discoverer of Philip's tomb, also excavated quite recently the theatre where the king was assassinated; it is small and at first sight undramatic; no stones were uncovered on the shallow tiers because it probably had wooden seats.

Also in the vicinity is a huge Iron Age cemetery, unmistakable because the area is bubbled with small tumuli.

Pella: Alexander the Great
From here the flattish road to Thessaloníki passes by Pella, birthplace of Alexander the Great (356 BC), until 148 BC, when it was sacked by the Romans, capital of Macedonia and linked to the sea by a canal. The site and museum are open daily until mid-afternoon. It is extensive: recent excavations on a low hill some two kilometres (one mile) from the site have uncovered a vast palace area with a courtyard, spacious rooms, a bathing-pool, and one side of a gigantic peristyle that was never completed. There is much else to be excavated; what can be seen on the site are a number of houses and adminstrative buildings with fine mosaic floors. Even more delicate mosaics are on display in the museum (closed on Tuesdays), along with exquisite clay votive figures and other finds.

Thessaloníki
Thessaloníki, approached across the flat delta, is Greece's second largest city (pop. c. 407,000), beautifully placed at the head of the

Northern Greece and the North Aegean

Thermaic Gulf. Founded at the end of the 4th century BC and named for Alexander the Great's half-sister, its importance grew with its strategic position on the Via Egnatia, linking Byzantium and Rome, until it became the second city of the Byzantine Empire. Its later history is one of seiges and sacks by Goths, Slavs, Saracens, Franks and Epirots; successive periods of Turkish occupation interspersed by a return to Byzantium and one spell as a Venetian protectorate, but culminating in nearly 500 years of Turkish rule which ended in 1912.

Five years later, fire destroyed much of the town, which was also damaged more recently by an earthquake in 1978. Its appearance is largely modern, forming a wide amphitheatre sloping down to the sea from the former Byzantine walls on the slopes of Mount Hortiatis, with a few crooked old streets beneath them. The centre of the city lies immediately behind the harbour and Nikis Avenue (formerly Leoforos Vasiléos Konstantinou), the seafront avenue that leads from the port area to the 15th century White Tower. Originally part of the city ramparts and scene of a Turkish massacre in 1826, it has now been converted to a Byzantine Museum (open daily, except Tuesdays, all day) with a small but fine collection, including icons, jewellery and tomb-frescoes, beautifully displayed. Parallel with Nikis, behind two pleasant waterfront squares (Plateia Elefthérias, and Plateia Aristotélous where the Tourist Information Office is) are the main arteries of the city: Megalou Alexandou Street (Tsimiski), Egnatías Street (which does not in fact follow the ancient Via Egnatia) and Aghiou Dhimitríou Street.

Towards its eastern end, Egnatías Street passes the 3rd century AD Arch of Galerius, a monument to the emperor's victory over the Persians, its fine reliefs somewhat overlaid by city grime. In the vast Plateia Dikastírion, between Egnatias and Aghiou Dhimitríou, part of the Roman Forum has been uncovered.

Byzantine Churches
The chief glory of Thessaloníki, however, is its Byzantine churches which, between them, span every period of Byzantine art and architecture. The oldest is Aghios Georgios, also called the Rotónda, a Roman brickwork rotunda temple of the late 3rd century, with mosaics in the dome; it has been a mosque as well as a church (a minaret still stands beside it) and is now a monument. Damaged in the 1978 earthquake, it has been under restoration since.

Next in chronological order is the Paraskeví, or Panaghia Acheiropoietos, an early (5th century) essay in the basilican form which has also been used as a mosque; it has been heavily restored. Aghios Dhimitrios, built at the end of the 5th century, is the largest and most perfect example of basilican form. Rebuilt, using original materials, after the 1917 fire, it retains many ancient features including 7th century mosaic panels on the columns flanking the opening of the apse. The crypt is original and tradition has it that miraculously-scented oil from the tomb of the saint (patron of the city) would flow down there from his tomb behind the altar. Aghia Sophia (8th century), with its distinctive green dome, has some interesting 9th-10th century mosaics in the dome.

Of the later churches, built on the "Greek Cross" plan, the oldest is the semi-sunken red brick Panaghia Khalkeon (11th century), opposite a Turkish bath in Plateia Dikastírion. Aghios Panteleimon (12th century) has been badly altered; Aghia Ekaterini (13th century) and Dhodekha Apostoloi (14th century, fine frescoes and mosaics) are the best-proportioned and visually most pleasing.

Museum and Ramparts

Thessaloníki also has an incredibly rich Archaeological Museum on the edge of a small park at the south-eastern end of the town (open daily, except Tuesdays, all day; shorter hours in winter). Particularly spectacular are the 4th century BC royal tomb finds, excavated from 1977 onwards by Professor Manolis Andronikos, discoverer of Philip II's tomb at Vergina and of others in the same tumulus, one still being excavated. The treasures on view include Philip's gold burial-casket and a smaller one, probably that of his wife Cleopatra; armour, ivories, lamps (including the earliest known storm-lantern); silver vessels inlaid with gold; wreaths in gold, and a staggering wealth of jewels. Equally spectacular are some of the finds from other Macedonian grave sites, including Dherveni and Sindos.

It is rewarding, especially in the evening when it is cool and the light over the gulf is particularly lovely, to climb to the ramparts and the little maze-like streets just below them; here is the tiny church of Ossios David (5th century) with an unusual mosaic of a beardless Saviour.

Shops

Thessaloníki is not as tourist-orientated as Athens, except in the Aristotélous Square area, and its shops are thus typically cosmopolitan. The main shopping streets are Ermou, parallel with Egnatias, while Eleftherou Venizélou which cuts across them is noted for fashions, particularly furs. The markets are off this latter street, a maze of fruit, vegetable and meat halls with the flower market just outside them, wrapped about a ruined Byzantine church just off Irakliou Street.

Restaurants and Hotels

Thessaloníki has a well-earned reputation for good food, and the grandest restaurant is Olympos-Naoussa on Nikis (open for lunch only; doors close at 1530). Near it is Stratis; also Ragias. *Tavernas* in the town centre include Klimataria, on Pavlou Mela, Spata on Aristotélous and Elvetiko on Aghias Sophias. An evenings-only *taverna* with music is To Sokaki in Kalapothaki. There are also good fish *tavernas* at

Aretsou and Nea Krini just outside town.

The nicest hotel was the elegant old Mediterranean Palace on the sea front, irreparably damaged in the 1978 earthquake. The Makedonia Palace, out beyond the White Tower, and the Electra Palace in Aristotélous are now the two top hotels. Among more modest ones are the Egnatia in Leontos Sofou and El Greco in Egnatias. *Kaffeneions* abound everywhere.

Festivals

An International Trade Fair followed by an Arts Festival and a popular music festival, run more or less uninterruptedly from mid-September each year until October 26th-28th. On October 26th is St Demetrios's Day, an important local festival; October 28th is of course a national holiday. It would be unwise to arrive during this period without hotel bookings.

Halkidikí Peninsula

Kassandra

The nearest bathing beach to the city is at the modest resort of Aghia Triada and its neighbourhood, a bus-ride away, but most tourists will choose to head further south, to the three-pronged Halkidikí peninsula, hilly, fertile and wooded. On the westernmost prong of Kassandra, much tourist development has taken place. Before crossing the narrow isthmus, site of ancient Potidaia, where another Macedonian tomb was discovered in 1984, two detours can be made. One, inland, is to the site of the ancient city of Olynthos, razed by Philip of Macedon in 348 though little of it is visible since the mosaics are usually covered over, the other is to the pretty little port town of Nea Moudanian, with inns and *tavernas*.

A road leads almost all round the Kassandra peninsula where there are large-scale hotel developments, not unattractive, and much used for package tours, particularly at Kassandras, Sani, Pallini and Kallithea. The prettiest part is Paliouri, at its tip, which has a Xenia hotel and a good camp site.

Sithonia

There is more development at the head of the gulf at Gerakini, en route to the lovely wooded Sithonia peninsula, the central one of the three, where the carefully-planned and imaginatively conceived new luxury resort of Porto Carras (hotels, villas) is centred on a newly-created marina and golf course in the neighbourhood of Neos Marmaras (itself rapidly expanding to cater for cheaper tourism). Otherwise, this peninsula is virtually deserted but for the Carras fruit and almond groves, vineyards and winery, olives and oil refinery; there are exquisite coves, a few pretty hamlets and the comparatively recently excavated 8th century BC site of Toróni, a short way further south.

Strymon Gulf

In the hills inland is Polyiros (pop. c. 5,200) chief town of Halkidikí; the road winds on north of it to join the main road from Thessaloníki to Stratonio on the Gulf of Strymon on the east coast. To the north of this attractive little port, a new and beautiful road winds up the coastline past long sandy beaches and charming villages, like Olympiada and Stavros, and bays set among pine woods; it cannot be long before this area starts to be more intensively developed.

Ierissós; Ouranoupolis

To the south, the main road continues along the lovely, undeveloped coast to Ierissós, an expanding resort beneath a mediaeval fortress, built on the site of ancient Akanthos. Several new hotels have gone up in the area beyond, where the road crosses the narrow isthmus across which Xerxes had a canal cut for the passage of his fleet. At the end of the road is Ouranoupolis (pop. c. 700), a busy little resort with several hotels, one of them the Xenia where wives traditionally stayed while their husbands made the pilgrimage to the Holy Mountain of Athos. Nowadays the wives can cruise along the west coast of the Athos peninsula from here, and view a selection of its monasteries through binoculars.

Mount Athos

Athos is said to have been reserved for worship by Our Lady, who landed here with St John en route from Palestine to Cyprus, and herself excluded all other women from visiting it. I cannot therefore write of it with first-hand experience, although I have taken the boat trip along the western shore. Men ("of provable religious and scientific interests") must obtain a permit for a visit through the consulate of their country of origin, either from the Foreign Ministry in Athens or the Ministry for Northern Greece in Thessaloníki. Permits are normally granted for stays of four days, though extensions can be made on the spot in Karyes, the administration centre and port at which the boats from Ouranoupolis land.

Travel round Athos is on foot or by mule, and hospitality, in the form of beds for the night and simple meals, which many people supplement by taking personal supplies of tinned food, is extended to visitors at each monastery; a contribution to monastery funds is expected in lieu of payment. It is highly inadvisable as well as impractical, I am told, to try to visit all twenty of the monasteries; one gets a better sense of the peace and contemplative nature of the place by spending a full day in each of a few of them.

Monastery Treasures

The following, briefly summarised, are among the most important.

Vathopedi: big and picturesque, mostly 17th century buildings around an 11th century basilica. It contains a precious relic — part of the Holy Girdle of Our Lady — and much treasure, notably the jasper and silver cup of Manuel Paleologos of Mistra. **Hiliandarí**: 12th century, with a patterned-brick Katolikon church containing 13th and 14th century frescoes. It possesses two precious ikons, a mosaic of the Virgin and Child and one of the Virgin with Three Hands, both 14th century. **Iviron**: 10th century with a fine big Katolikon church and a later chapel containing the miraculous Portaítissa ikon, painted by St Luke and rescued from the sea by a monk who was allowed to walk upon its surface to do so. **Grand Lavra**: founded by St Athanasius in the 10th century, it is the biggest and least-damaged of all the monasteries, with 16th century Cretan frescoes and a rich treasury and library. **Xenophóntos**: 10th century with later Cretan frescoes and ikons, and 14th century mosaics. **Docheriou**: 10th century and one of the most attractive architecturally, it has a splendid Katolikon with Cretan frescoes. **Aghios Dionysiou**: though of later date (14th century), Robert Liddell calls this "the most . . . satisfying monastery on the whole mountain". **Zográphou**: buildings mostly modern, but it contains another miraculous ikon, that of St George.

Both Robert Liddell in 'Mainland Greece' and Patrick Leigh Fermor in 'Roumeli' have written interestingly and at length about Athos monasteries and they are, of course, fully described in the Benn 'Blue Guide' to Greece and the Collins 'Companion Guide to Mainland Greece'.

North and East of Thessaloníki

The Strymon Valley
North and East of Halkidikí is the broad Strymon valley, at one time the boundary of Macedonia and Thrace. Serres, overlooking the valley from the centre of its eastern rim, is an attractive, shady town dominated by a ruined 14th century *kastro*; it stands near the junction of the main road into Bulgaria.

As this road approaches Thessaloníki, there is a turning off to the east to Langadhás, largest of the handful of villages, where on May 21st, the day of SS Constantine and Helen, the *Anastenaria* fire-walking dances take place. They continue for two more days and are supposed to have originated when the saints' ikons were rescued from fire in the 13th century, but may have much earlier — even pagan — origins. Nowadays, however, the ceremonies are unaffectedly religious in character, in no way "adapted" for tourist consumption (though Langadhás, being so close to Thessaloníki, is accustomed to seeing spectators arrive), and curiously moving. Nearer to Thessaloníki is the Dherveni grave site from which came the rich finds now in the archaeological museum.

Amphipolis
The main highway to the east runs along a wide valley parallel with
two huge lakes: Koronia which is shallow, and Volvi, steeper-sided
and more scenic. It more or less follows the course of the ancient
Via Egnatia, crossing the River Strymon beneath the gaze of the huge
restored statue of the Lion of Amphipolis. The ruins of the city —
once a station on the Via Egnatia through which St Paul passed, and
before that a wealthy city in Classical times — are slightly inland,
poorly signposted. They lie on a freely accessible grassy hill with
widespreading views: remains of two early Christian basilicas with
mosaic pavements, a scatter of other unidentified ruins and fallen
column capitals, silent and largely ignored. The main road continues
through a dramatic cleft at the foot of Mount Pangaion, and forks left
(for Drama) just before Kavála.

Philippi
Some eight kilometres (five miles) to the north are the ruins of Philippi
(open daily, all day; museum closed on Tuesdays). These seem to
occupy an inconspicuous position on a low hillside until one reaches
them and once again realises with what genius the ancient Greeks
sited their cities, for Philippi in fact commands the whole plain.
Although it dates back to the 6th century BC, it did not become
important until the Roman era, when it was refounded after the Battle
of Philippi (42 BC) in which Antony and Octavian defeated the forces
of Brutus and Cassius. The city then became a prosperous stage on
the Via Egnatia, and most of the older ruins are Roman, principally a
Forum, below the road, and a remodelled Theatre above it. In AD 49
St Paul made his first sermons on European soil here and Philippi
became robustly Christian; among the excavations are the remains
of two 6th century basilicas, a public latrine, and the agora. The
museum displays a good collection of finds; the theatre is used for
summer festivals.

Kavala
Back on the main road, the route twists upwards through a narrow
pass in the hills and suddenly Kavala and, beyond it, the shining
expanse of the northern Aegean come into view from the top. There
are splendid views, as one winds downward again, of this handsome
town which rises gently from a broad waterfront into the slopes
behind. Kavala (pop. c. 55,000) has a number of good hotels, mostly
grouped around the Eleftherias Square at the centre of the waterfront
and excellent restaurants on the quayside itself. It is an important
bus terminal and a departure point for ferry boats to Thassos.

The older part of town, its Byzantine walls still standing, occupies a
small promontory at the eastern end of the quay; stretching towards
it are the remains of a grandiose Turkish aqueduct. Strongly Turkish
in character, it is dominated by the crumbling Imaret (almshouse)
with its many cupolas, a mosque and a hammam. Mehmet Ali, king

95

of Egypt and a forbear of the deposed late King Farouk, was born here; his palace (complete with harem) is near the belvedere at the tip of the promontory. There is also a small museum (open daily, except Tuesdays, until mid-afternoon) at the western end of the quayside in the modern town.

Kavala to Alexandroupolis
The eastbound road passes above the local bathing beaches and beach hotels and curves inland. A branch to the right runs across the flat, alluvial plain through villages, where a few storks still nest, to the little port of Kermaotí (inns and *tavernas*). This is the terminal for the shortest ferry route (20 minutes) to the island of Thassos.

After Keramotí turn-off, the road runs through the narrow strip of Thrace that separates Bulgaria from the Mediterranean, linking towns and villages that become increasingly Turkish in character and appearance. The first is Xanthi (pop. c. 31,000) from which there are two alternative roads: the main one loops to the seaward side of Lake Vistonida, crossing a narrow spit of land between the two and passing through the small port of Lagos.

Komotiní
The secondary road is straighter and follows the inland route of the Via Egnatia. Both join just before Komotiní (pop. c. 37,000) with the largest Turkish community in Greece. At first sight uninteresting, it is nevertheless a convenient stop (good hotels) on the road to Istanbul, and an evening stroll about town reveals unexpected charms: several mosques, a semi-derelict *hammam*, Turkish-looking streets and a large central square with *tavernas* and *kaffenions*.

The last sizeable town before the border is Alexandroupolis, (pop. c. 35,000) a pleasant modern port town with several good motels and hotels and ferries to Samothraki and Lemnos. Beyond it is the Evros delta, rich in bird life; northwards by some 60 kilometres (38 miles) is the small silk-manufacturing town of Soufli (pop. c. 5,500). Eastwards lies Turkey, across the Evros.

North Aegean Islands

Thassos
The three principal northern Aegean islands are Thassos, Lemnos and Samothraki. Closest to the coast, Thassos was famous in antiquity for its gold mines and its timber, much in demand for shipbuilding. A round blob of an island that rises to a point at the centre, most of Thassos is thickly wooded, and this verdance gives it a special beauty.

Limin
The ferries from Kavala and Keramotí land at the quayside of the

little capital, Limin, built on the site of the ancient town, many of whose extensive ruins are engagingly muddled up with the buildings of the modern town, which has several hotels. There is a small museum (open daily, except Tuesdays, until mid-afternoon) to one side of it, and almost fronting the ancient harbour (still used by fishing boats), is the Agora (same hours as the museum) dating from Archaic times but reconstructed by the Romans. Behind this are traces of the Roman road and Odeum. The older, Classical ruins (fragments of bas reliefs) lie parallel with the foreshore to the east of the Agora and behind, where there is a 4th century BC theatre set into the steep slope leading up the Acropolis (foundations of a temple, remains of a Genoese castle). The ancient city walls can be followed all round the area — a stiff walk.

Other villages
Bus services make a complete circuit of the island, running inland through forests only on the east flank where the coast is precipitous. Before turning into the hills they pass the Makriámmos Beach Hotel and then rejoin the coast at Potamiá (hotels, *tavernas*). The southern end of the island is more barren and typically Aegean than the north: its principal village is Limenária, straggling attractively along a series of little inlets backed by olive groves (modest hotels).

Samothraki
Samothraki is on a ferry route from Kymi to Alexandroupolis and back and is linked by ferry to Kavála. Ruggedly bare, windy and wave-beaten, with a few hotels (summer only) Samothraki was in ancient times a strategic port of call between Asia Minor and Greece, and also possessed a strong navy. It has strong legendary and historic associations: Poseidon is supposed to have observed the progress of the Trojan War from its heights and Troy itself may well have been founded from there. It provided Philip of Macedon with his wife, the mother of Alexander the Great; saw the death of Perseus of Macedon; and was visited by St Paul en route to Philippi.

Samothraki Town
The little capital, Samothraki, stands in the hills above the harbour beneath a mediaeval fort. The ruins of the important and exceedingly ancient Sanctuary of the Great Gods, where in 1864 French archaeologists unearthed the Wingless Victory, now in the Louvre, lies at Paleopolis on the north coast a short distance from the port.

Lemnos
Lemnos is also served by ferries from Alexandroupolis and Kavála, and has a small airport. Rivalling Samothraki in antiquity, it was the legendary home of the fire god Hephaistos who wooed Aphrodite there; its women then incurred Aphrodite's displeasure and she cursed

them, causing them to murder their husbands. They were conveniently replaced by some of Jason's companions from the *Argo*, which called there soon after this deed. Historically Lemnos, which traditionally ranged itself on the side of Athens, was frequently prey to the Persians during the Persian Wars. In time it became an important outpost of Byzantium, then fell to Venice, and finally to Turkey, from which it was freed after World War I. A famous Allied naval base was established during that war in its natural harbour of Moudros Bay on the south coast — which, together with Pournia Bay on the north coast, almost splits the island in two.

Myrina; Moudros Bay
The capital is the little townlet of Myrina in the west, dominated by a castle; there is a small museum, and a luxury bungalow hotel on the adjacent beach. Linked to Myrina by road are the seaside villages around Moudros Bay. The island's most important archaeological site, Poliochni, which dates back to earliest Neolithic times, is near the village of Kaminia, a few kilometres from Moudros.

Ifestia and Chloi
Ifestia, the ancient capital on the north shore, is traditionally the spot on which the fire-god landed, crippling himself, when his parents Zeus and Hera flung him from Olympos for interfering in one of their arguments. Both it and nearby Chloi (a sanctuary where fertility rites for women were performed; explicit votives had been excavated) retain vestiges of their ancient past.

Parga

Western Greece
and the
Ionian Islands

Western Greece

Western Greece is virtually isolated from the rest of the country by the massive Pindos range, which is crossed by only two good roads, one from Ioannina that loops north and east to Kozani, the other more direct, from Ioannina to Metsovo and Trikala. It is rugged and mountainous country, with a less civilised early history than its neighbour states: only Aetolia, the most southwesterly of its three provinces, sent forces to the Trojan War. In Hellenistic times (3rd century BC), a strong Aetolian League defied the invading Gauls and ruled much of the territory to the north of the Gulf of Corinth, before falling to Macedonia. Epirus, the northernmost province, was for long a kingdom ruled by the Molossi tribe; its most famous king was Pyrrhus whose short-lived unprofitable triumphs over Macedon and Rome in the 3rd century BC have given us the term "Pyrrhic victory".

In Byzantine times, much of Western Greece was parcelled with what are now Albania and southern Yugoslavia; it became a despotate in the Middle Ages and thereafter was ruled partly by the Turks and partly by Venice. In recent time much of Northern Epiros has belonged to Albania and thousands of Greeks still live on the "wrong" side of the border.

Around Igoumenitsa and Parga

To travellers approaching Greece on the car ferry from southern Italy, Western Greece is the gateway to the country, with the port of Igoumenitsa as its front door; it is therefore logical to cover the area from that starting point. Igoumenitsa itself (pop. c. 6,000) is a cheerful polyglot township with a number of hotels and *tavernas* ranged along and behind its waterfront, all well geared to the needs of transient motorists. For their convenience, also, the southbound road is being ambitiously re-engineered to shorten the distance to the Corinthian Gulf and the Athens highway. Plans for a motorway eastwards across the country to Volos are still embryonic.

Parga

Parga (pop. c. 2,000), which has for some years been experiencing fairly tactful tourist development, is one of the most picturesque seaside towns in all Greece, sprawled along a magnificent double-head bay beneath a promontory topped with a Norman *kastro*. The smaller bay, studded with rocks and tiny islets, is lined with *tavernas* and *kaffeneions*; behind it the town slopes gently uphill, a maze of narrow streets lined with small hotels and pensions, shops and *kaffeneions*. The larger bay has a splendid beach and the more recent tourist development spreading inland behind it.

To the south and east of Parga the river Acherontas, one of the ancient arteries of the Underworld, flows into the sea from the mountainous region behind Glíki, once the stronghold of the fiercely independent Suliot tribe; the remote vestiges of the Castle of Suli stands high above the river gorge. When the Suliots were forced to flee from the Turkish governor, Ali Pasha, many of them escaped through Parga, to the Ionian islands, then in French hands.

It would be hard to resist spending at least a few nights in Parga and, with so many interesting things in the neighbourhood, there are several reasons for doing so. Not least of them is the total lack, so far, of any major development along the coast south of it, which must have some of the finest beaches in the country. This pristine state of affairs will certainly change when the new road is finished,

Right: Roasting Easter lambs. Lion at Dilos (top).
Samothraki, Sanctuary of the Great Gods (below).
Overleaf: Boatbuilding at Kithira (top).
The Aesklepion, Kos (below).

so is worth enjoying now while there is the chance.

Necromanteion Efiras

Just inland of the seaside village of Ammoudia, near Messopotamo, a sanctuary stood on the banks of the Acherontas to which the ancients would come to communicate, through an oracle, with the dead. A series of gloomy chambers and passages, both above and beneath the ground, the Necromanteion Efiras, was excavated there some 30 years ago. The huge alluvial plain between it and the sea at Ammoudia was once the lagoon, fed by the Acherontas, across which the legendary ferryman Charon steered souls into the river-gorge to the mouth of Hades.

Kassopi and Nikópolis

Some 28 kilometres (17 miles) further south, up in the hills behind the road to Arta, are the extensive remains of Kassopi (open daily until mid-afternoon), a city founded in the 4th century BC; an agora with part of a portico, an odeon and the base of a public building have been uncovered. Not far is the monastery of Zalongo where a band of Suliot women hurled themselves and their children off the cliff rather than fall into the hands of Ali Pasha's soldiers; a modern group of sculptures commemorates them.

About 13 kilometres (8 miles) further south again are the widespread remnants of Nikópolis, founded by the Roman Emperor Augustus (Octavian) after the defeat of Anthony and Cleopatra at the Battle of Actium (Akteion) in 31 BC; he sacked Kassopi (see above) and drove out its citizens in order to populate it. There are miles of walls, mostly Byzantine; a theatre, an odeon, the remains of a temple and of two basilicas. St Paul is said to have preached at Nikopolis, but the oldest basilica post-dates him by five centuries; the newer one, built in the 6th century AD, retains some floor mosaics. Traces of the triumphal monument Augustus built to celebrate his victory can be seen beyond the theatre. There is also a small museum, normally open until mid-afternoon except on Tuesdays, and several *tavernas* nearby.

Preveza

Preveza (pop. c. 12,500) is just a few kilometres further south, on the strait that connects the Ambracian Gulf (Amvrakikos Kolpos) with the sea, and linked to Akteion, the opposite promontory, (and to its own airport) by a ferry. When the new west coast road is finished and the bridge built across the strait, Preveza will become a mainline town; now it is quiet and pleasant, if unremarkable, with several hotels,

Previous page: Santorini (left). The old town, Rhodes (right).
Near Kavala, northern Greece (below).
Left: Street scene (top). Ios town (below).

fish *tavernas* on the quayside, and a *kastro* from which there are splended views out over the Ionian.

The new road will also relieve pressure on the beautiful but winding inland route that heads into the mountains from Igoumenitsa and for part of the way follows the tortuous course of the Kalamas river before coming out on to the high plateau of Ioannina.

Ioannina

This charming lakeside town (pop. c. 45,000, capital of Epiros) has good hotels including a Xenia, many restaurants, *tavernas* and open-air *kaffenions* in its town-centre gardens and along the lake shore, and a surprising amount of car-parks. It also boasts an airport and the bus terminal for routes covering most of Western Greece. It is ringed by fields of corn and tobacco plantations stretching over a plain hedged about by purplish mountains, the highest being the peaks of the Pindos to the east.

It is not an ancient city: although founded by the Emperor Justinian in the 6th century, it did not become important until the 13th century when its Byzantine despots (governors) made it a centre of ecclesiastical art. Its most notorious ruler, however, was the cruel and licentious Albanian-born Ali Pasha whose allegiance was theoretically to Turkey but more accurately to himself: he established his capital here and made a name for himself throughout Europe until his death in 1820 after an unsuccessful revolt against the Ottoman Sultan. Byron, who arrived in Ioannina in 1809 to find him absent, immediately rode for more than a week over the mountains into Albania to visit him, so lurid was his reputation.

One of the two spots particularly associated with Ali Pasha is the quayside where nearly a score of loose ladies of the town were tipped into the lake in sacks (Ali Pasha himself was more interested in boys). The other is the island in the middle of the lake where Ali was finally killed by the soldiers of the Sultan. His death took place in Aghios Panteleimonos, one of the half dozen pretty monasteries that adorn the island in the lake. The room in which he was killed, still marked with bullet-holes and hung with photographs (of Byron, among others), can be visited.

Citadel and Museums

The town itself stands above the lake shore, to which it slopes down from Pirou Square, bisected by the broad, main Dodonis Avenue and flanked by gardens full of café tables. At one end is the museum (open daily, except Tuesdays, until mid-afternoon) with votives from Dodona and Necromantia, and Byzantine objects. On the eastern edge, there are fine views from the bastions. The Odos Averof, lined with shops selling the traditional silver filigree work, runs down from this vantage point to the stubby walled peninsula of the citadel, or *frourio*, site of the despots' stronghold and of Ali Pasha's own headquarters. The *frourio* was once separated from the land by a moat but this is now filled in. It is a picturesque quarter of old houses, many being carefully restored, and others being built in the traditional style. At the eastern tip is the inner *frourio* with Ali Pasha's palace (being transformed into a museum); his tomb and a mosque. Further north, the Aslan Pasha Mosque is now a museum of Epirot arts and crafts (open daily except Tuesdays until mid-afternoon), with a minaret alongside it. There are fine lake views from the terrace and behind it are the Old Synagogue and restored Turkish Library. The lakeside promenade outside the walls of the *kastro* are pleasantly shady and from it boats cross regularly to the island, where there are fish *tavernas;* these are the places in which to try the local Zitsa wine.

Ioannina to Konitsa; Zagoria

Mount Smolikas

From Ioannina northwards to Konitsa and beyond there is more than enough to occupy a day's exploration. Serious walkers and climbers will need more time than this if they want to tackle Mount Smolikas and its wild surroundings; on the Pass of the same name is a simple, rustic restaurant where a wood-fire burns in all but the high summer months and the skin of a bear, shot only a couple of years ago, hangs on the wall. Further east, towards Siatitsa, at the summit of the Pendalofos Pass, the small stone-built eponymous hamlet was the headquarters of the British Mission to the Greek Resistance in World War II. Devotees of caves should certainly spare an hour or so for the Perama Cave (open day-long, guided tours) just 6 kilometres (under 4 miles) north of Ioannina. It was discovered early in World War II when the townspeople were looking for possible bomb-shelter and has now been illuminated. The views from the outside are superb.

Vikos Gorge

Konitsa itself, just off the road some 65 kilometres (40 miles) north of Ioannina, is an old village of much charm on the edge of the National Park that encompasses the Vikos Gorge and much of the mountainous and thickly wooded Zagoria country, where the Greeks held off the invading Italians in 1940. The turnoff to the northern end of the gorge is signposted to Aristi and Papingo, a dramatically hair-pinning road, mostly metalled, up through the scattered, stone-built hamlet of Aristi. Beyond it one arm of a fork leads up to the remote community of Papingo (where the National Tourist Organisation has restored several houses for letting); the other ends at the top of the gorge, at Vikos, from which it is possible to make the steep descent into the gorge itself. Some way along it, recent excavations have yielded traces of a paleolithic people who lived there between 10,000 and 16,000 year ago.

The other approach to the Vikos Gorge is from Astaka, closer to Ioannina, by another well-surfaced road that hairpins up through the hamlets of Vitsa and Monodendri, both with many of the area's typical grey stone houses. Beyond Monodendri the Monastery of Aghia Peraskevi seems to hang from the edge of the 1,000-foot precipice rearing up from the gorge, and from there a precarious path leads to the bottom.

Ioannina to Arta

Dodona

South of Ioannina a by-road off the main highway winds steeply into the wild hills, seemingly headed for nowhere, and suddenly emerges into a small friendly-looking valley at the centre of which are the dramatic ruins of Dodona, or Dodoni (open daily, except Tuesdays, all day), where a drama festival is held each August. Site of the most ancient oracle in Greece and founded, it is said, when twin doves from Thebes settled here and at Ammon in what is now Libya, Dodona is one of the most evocative ruins in the country. The god Zeus spoke here through water, earth and the whispering oak leaves, and although the great groves no longer exist, there are still oak trees and the place seems to echo faintly with murmured prophecies. Odysseus was one of those to whom the oracle spoke. There is a beautifully restored theatre, bigger even than that of Epidavros, to which the entire valley and the surrounding mountains are a backdrop; beside it are the foundations of the sanctuary and temples and an early Christian basilica, and behind it rises the acropolis hilltop.

Louros Gorge

From the Dodona turnoff, the southbound road runs straight over the plain at first and then enters the wooded Louros gorge (*tavernas* and *kaffeneions*) skirts the Louros Dam and emerges near Filippiada where there is a large orangeade factory edging the orange groves of the Ambracian plain. Here it forks, the right fork leading round the north shore of the Ambracian Gulf to Preveza.

At present this is a long detour from the main southbound highway but the bridge that will one day cross the strait will complete the new coastal road from Igoumenitsa down to Messolonghi. Now, however, southbound motorists in a hurry should fork left after Filippiada for Arta.

Arta

An attractive, lively town of no small historical and artistic interest, Arta is approached across the Arakhthos near the famous, gracefully-arched bridge into which, so legend has it, "the fair wife of John, the foremost master-builder" was interred in the early 17th century — to appease the evil influence which had repeatedly caused the central arch to collapse.

Arta, (pop. c. 18,000) built on the site of ancient Ambracia, Pyrrhus's capital, has two or three hotels including a Xenia built into the walls of the 13th century *frourio*, or castle.

Churches
It also has several important churches. The eccentrically-shaped Aghia Theodora convent church is dedicated to the virtuous wife of the mediaeval despot Michael Commenus II who, when turned out by her husband and his mistress, the sorceress Lady Gangrene, became a nun here and was later canonised. Aghios Vasilios, near it, has a decorative brickwork exterior. The most important of Arta's churches is the huge multi-domed 13th century Panaghia Paragorítissa with a curiously complicated interior construction in which antique columns have been used, and an impressive mosaic Pantocrator.

Kato Panaghia
Just outside the town to the south is the little nunnery of Kato Panaghia, where rugs are woven and sold; it was built by Michael II in thanksgiving his eventual deliverance from the Lady Gangrene's spells. On the other side of the river to the north is the monastery of Moni Vlachernai, embellished by Michael II whose supposed tomb it contains.

Arta to Messolonghi
Amfilokhia; Vonitsa; Akteion
South of Arta the road runs through orange groves to the eastern shore of the Ambracian Gulf which it skirts in a miniature *corniche* before coming to Amfilokhia (pop. c. 4,200) a little town cradled between the steep sides of the narrow inlet it commands. It has inns and *tavernas* and a branch road that runs along the south side of the gulf through Vónitsa to the Castle of Grivas near Akteion (Actium), connecting with the ferry from Preveza and eventually leading to the island of Lefkas.

If there is time to dawdle a bit, take this road and turn south at Vónitsa to follow the coast for 40 kilometres (25 miles). As yet totally unspoiled (development will come when the bridge at Preveza is built), it is a succession of beautiful coves and beaches with a few resort hamlets. The largest (pop. c. 2,700) is Astakós, with small inns; ferries operate from there to Ithaca and Kefallonia.

Stratos and the Aetolian Lakes
The main road continues south, past the lakes of Ambrakia and Ozeros, through tobacco plantations and wild scenery to cross the Akheloos dam. On a bluff above it are the ruins of the classical city of Stratos; its great walls loom up beside the road but much of it still lies buried

except for a blue-grey Doric temple of Zeus on the westernmost periphery of the site.

South of it is Agrinion (pop. c. 35,000), a modern busy tobacco-industry town with an airport and hotels at the dead centre of a tobacco growing area. A beautiful mountain road runs north and east up to the huge, many-fingered Kremastón dam (lakeside *tavernas*) and on beneath Mount Timfristós to Karpenísi. The main southbound road runs along a narrow spit between two lakes: the smaller Lake Lysimakhia to the west and Lake Trichonis to the east. A secondary road runs around this latter lake, the northern shore of which is delightfully shady and shelters a few hamlets. At the easternmost extremity are the ruins of ancient Thermon, not a city but the administrative centre and religious meeting place of the Aetolians; its remains are complicated to follow, since they are mixed with very much earlier ones, but the most notable building is the narrow temple of the Thermian Apollo, dating from the 6th century BC.

The main road, which can be rejoined from the south shore of the lake continues south through a mountain pass towards Aetóliko, (pop. c. 4,200) crowded on to an islet between two lagoons and tethered to the mainland at either end by arched causeways. This is where the coastal road from Astakós rejoins the main inland one, passing the walled ruins of ancient Oeniadhe near the village of Katohí.

Pleuron
South of Aetoliko the main road follows the line of the Messolonghi lagoon, running between grainfields and olive groves and salt flats, with the "Kastro Kyria Irini" — in fact the immense tower-studded walls of ancient Pleuron, built in the 3rd century BC — dominating the view from a hilly spur. The climb up to it is stiff but the view from it magnificent, and among the scattered ruins (to the south-west) is that of a tiny theatre, said to be the smallest in Greece.

Messolonghi to the Gulf of Corinth
Messolonghi (Missolonghi, pop. c. 10,000) is clearly a place of pilgrimage for English speaking people, but is likely to disappoint those who expect it to look as romantic as its associations. A sprawling modern provincial town with a couple of new hotels, and restaurants and *kaffeneions,* it sits on the shore of a huge melancholy lagoon dotted with fish-hatcheries and animated by the swoop of wild birds and the soundless gliding motion of flat-bottomed boats. Its background is the foothills of Varasova.

Byron and Greek Independence
Messolonghi's fame, out of all proportion to its appearance, is of course due to the heroic death here of the Grecophile poet, Lord Byron. He came in January 1824, bringing not only the prestige of his name

but also funds from English well-wishers (including himself) for the cause of Greek independence and found the leaders dispirited and demoralised in an apparently hopeless situation that was not improved by the wintry weather. He could have left in disgust and despair, but instead he stayed, his heroism manifesting itself not in any romantic form but in a dogged patience entirely foreign to his nature. He caught a chill, developed a severe fever — probably malaria, but the mosquitoes have now been eradicated — and resigned himself to an unpleasant death, miserable and lonely but setting an example that re-animated the entire cause. It was not until 1828 that the town was eventually liberated, after three punitive sieges. One of these, the 1826 *Exodos,* in which the people attempting to break out were slaughtered, is commemorated annually on April 23.

Byron's statue, beneath which the poet's heart is buried, is in the pleasant garden of the Heroon (Heroes Garden), flanked by the tomb of the Suliot soldier Votsaris, and by a mound topped by an improbable memorial containing the bodies of unnamed dead. There is a little Revolution Museum in the *Dimarcheion* (town hall) in the main square (open daily until early afternoon). The house where Byron died, which was destroyed by an Italian bomb in World War II, has been replaced by a memorial garden.

Kalydon and Evinos
From Messolonghi the main road runs eastwards and inland of Mount Varasova to the village of Evihokhori, from which a track leads up to the site of ancient Kalydon with a tremendous view. Its legend, retold in Swinburne's tragedy *Atalanta in Calydon*, concerns Meleager, son of Oeneus, whose lands were ravaged by a wild boar. Atalanta came from Arcadia to join the hunt for it and when Meleager slew it, he offered it to her. This caused a quarrel with his uncles, whom Meleager then killed and his mother, in her fury, rekindled the brand on the continued existence of which the Fates had decreed Meleager's own life depended, and Meleager himself died. The ruins include the sanctuary of Artemis Laphria, dating from the 4th century BC, where live animals were sacrificed.

The highway then crosses the Evinos river, where the centaur Nessos, carrying Herakles' wife, tried to ravish her and was killed by her husband. As he was dying, Nessos persuaded the lady to dip a shirt in his blood which, he said, would keep Herakles true to her; in fact it was poisonous and when she later gave it to Herakles to wear, he died.

A few miles further, the road emerges on to a dramatic corniche above the entrance to the Gulf of Corinth, giving marvellous views of Kefallonia and the Peloponnese, and then dips to Antirio, gateway either to the Peloponnese (by car ferry to Rio) or the Central Greece (via Nafpaktos, Amphissa and Delphi.)

111

The Ionian Islands

The Ionians, also known in Greek as the Eptánisa (Seven Islands) include Corfu, Paxos, Lefkas, Ithaka, Kefalonia, Zakinthos or Zante and, oddly enough, Kithira at the southermost tip of the Peloponnese. The first six are the tips of a sunken limestone mountain range that parallels the coast of Western Greece and have throughout their history been subject to volcanic disturbance. They are temperate and lush by Greek standards, with rainy winters.

Historically, Ithaka is the most important, as the home of Odysseus, and Homer also refers to the islands of Doulichion, Same and Zakynthos as having sent ships to Troy. Same has been identified as Kefalonia and Zakynthos of course as Zante, but Doulichon is still the subject of learned wrangle: it may even have sunk in an earthquake. The islands figure little in ancient history after Homer; originally colonised by Corinth, they fell into Roman hands in the 3rd century BC and were subsequently Byzantine possessions until, in the 13th century, the Venetians took them and held them until the end of the 18th century — Italian is still widely spoken. They then passed to France; only very briefly to Turkey, having in fact been a bulwark of Christendom during the Turkish occupation of the rest of Greece; back to Napoleonic France again and, from 1815, were for nearly 50 years a British protectorate.

Corfu

Corfu or Kerkira, known as Corcyra to the ancients and, before that, Skheria or "at the end of the earth", is the most northerly of the Ionian islands, held by many to be the most beautiful, and certainly the best known and most popular. It has an international airport and is also a staging post on the Brindisi-Patras car ferry routes (stopovers permitted). Mountainous in the north, where it parallels the Albanian coast, and flatter in the south, it has one of the densest rural populations (c. 98,000) in Greece, partly by reason of its fertility: olives and fruit grow in profusion, though tourism now outstrips agriculture as the island's source of income and employment. Snakes are not uncommon — mostly harmless. A local speciality is the Kumquat, or *Kum-kwat,* miniature oranges which are crystallised as sweets, or made into a sweet liqueur.

History
In legend, Corfu is identified with Homeric Skheria, island Kingdom of the Phaecians, where Odysseus was shipwrecked after escaping from Calypso and succoured by Nausicaa, the King's daughter. Historically, it is noteworthy as the site of the first Greek naval battle, in the 7th century BC, when the Corinthian colony there rose against the mother city; a later uprising against Corinth in the 5th century

BC, when Athens sided with Corfu, sparked off the Peloponnesian War. In later times it was Roman (Octavian set out from here for the Battle of Actium, and Nero was a visitor) and Byzantine; Richard Coeur de Lion of England also passed through it on his return from the Crusades. Its chief visible legacies, however, are from its long Venetian past: it escaped the ravages of the 1953 earthquake and, although its capital was damaged during World War II, much of its Venetian flavour remains.

Corfu Town

The capital, Corfu or Kerkira (pop c. 34,000), though heavily tourist-orientated, is an elegant town with tall old houses, narrow streets and arcaded sidewalks centred around a tree-shaded esplanade, the Spianadha, with a bandstand and "cricket ground" (a British legacy); it was once the military parade-ground of the Venetians. To seaward of it is the walled citadel, or Palaio Frourio (open daily until mid-afternoon; *son et lumière* in summer). Separated from the mainland by a moat, it contains Venetian fortifications, a minute harbour and a former British garrison church. Along the landward or eastern edge of the Spianadha runs the Liston, a row of arcaded houses including *tavernas* and *kaffeneion,* built under Napoleon in imitation of the rue de Rivoli in Paris. At its northern end is the Old Palace of St Michael and St George, now partly a museum of Oriental Art, open daily except Tusdays until mid-afternoon. Alongside it, the town rises steeply in a tangle of chasmic alleyways flanked by tall houses towards the half-ruined and overgrown Neo Frourio. Below this, to the north, lie the main harbour and Customs buildings.

St Spiridon

The present-day heart of Corfu town lies behind Kapodistríou Street (named after the first President of independent Greece, who was a Corfiot), which parallels the Liston, and particularly in the 17th century Church of Aghios Spiridon. St Spiridon is the patron saint of Corfu and enjoys an unusually close relationship with his people: he is credited with several important miracles to their benefit, the most recent having been during World War II when he caused an Allied bomb to explode in mid-air before it actually hit his church and the hundreds who were sheltering in it. Beautifully embalmed and preserved in a handsome glass-fronted silver coffin, he is paraded in the streets four times a year (Palm Sunday, Easter Saturday, August 11 and the first Sunday in November) and is an object of extreme veneration: two out of every three Corfiot boys are called Spiro. Unfortunately his church does not do him justice, in aesthetic terms. Nearby is the busy fruit and vegetable market and the main pedestrian thoroughfare, Nikiforou Theotoki Street, which runs down towards the port.

Garitsa Bay

The newest part of town stretches southwards along Garitsa Bay;

Western Greece and the Ionian Islands

here are most of the hotels: the Corfu Palace in the luxury class and the A class Cavalieri are both to be recommended. Also in the modern town is the Archaelogical Museum (open daily, except Tuesdays, until mid-afternoon) with Archaic, Classical and Hellenistic finds from various parts of the island.

At the southernmost end of Garitsa Bay, just inland, is the 12th century Byzantine church of Aghi Iasonos kai Sosipatros; further south again is the Royal Villa of Mon Repos where the Duke of Edinburgh was born and, inland of it, a ruined basilica built on ancient foundations and incorporating Classical masonry. This is the site of the original city of which only vestiges remain; its acropolis is occupied by the village of Analipsis, which crowns a promontory bordered on the landward side by a vast lagoon and the airport. At the tip of the promontory, heavily built over with hotels and apartments, is the former Napoleonic gun battery of Kanoni, now festooned with café tables, from which one gets the much-photographed view of the two islet-monasteries of Vlakhernia and Pondikonisi.

South to Korission
South of the lagoon and airport are Benitses and Perama and the village of Gastouri, above which is the 19th century Italianate villa (now a casino) and gardens of the Achilleion, built for the Empress Elisabeth of Austria. Southwards again, the road winds along the coast past villas and hotels packed between the hills and the sea; inland, among the pine woods, another parallel road leads through Aghoi Dekha (attractive village, wonderful views) and along the heights. They join where the narrow southern strip of the island flattens out, near Messonghi. There is one cluster of low hills crowned by the village of Khlomos and the great lagoon of Korission; for the rest, olive and fruit groves and salt pans predominate, tended by the inhabitants of several large villages; there are also some fine beaches and several package tour hotels.

North-East Corfu
North of Corfu town the main road keeps to the plain on the eastern side of the island where the neighbourhoods of Gouvia Bay, Dassia and Ipsos are heavily built up; the asphalt and development thins after Pirghí. From here a road follows the north-east coast along a corniche through several little villages to Nissaki and Kouloura, with views of the hills screening the huge salt lagoon of Butrinto, now in Albania. In legend, Andromache, widow of Hector of Troy, ended her days there; it was also said by the Crusaders to have been the birthplace of Judas Iscariot. More prosaically, it has always been rich in fish and wildfowl; Ali Pasha, the Turkish ruler of Epiros, went there to hunt.

Farther along the coast (much visited by day-trippers by boat) is the pretty little resort of Kassiopi where stood the famous Temple of

Zeus that Nero came to Corfu to visit.

Another rough road from Pirghí climbs the towering Pantokrator mountain with its 14th century monastery, now dominated by a television mast and relay station. However, there are superb views: Butrinto can be seen even more clearly from this vantage-point.

North-West Corfu
To reach the north-west part of the island one forks left at Gouvia, and after a few miles the road forks again. The right-hand prong goes due north, through the handsome village of Skripero and down to Karousadhes from which the seaside resorts of Rodha (to the east) and Sidari (to the west) are both accessible. Another fork to the left leads to the resort of Aghios Geórgios.

The left-hand fork crosses the island in a westerly direction, passing beneath the hill village of Lakones (marvellous views from the Bella Vista café, just outside it), dominated by the ruins of the 13th century Angelokastro. It then winds down to the bay of Palaokastritsa, once famous for its peace, beauty and lobsters, now overbuilt with hotels and villas. Paleokastritsa is also reached more directly from Corfu town via Daniliá, "the village" — a reconstruction, for tourists' benefit, of the traditional Corfiot way of life that mass-tourism has put an end to.

Another generous bay on the west coast of Corfu is that of Glyfada, now reached by a good road that cuts straight across the island through the village of Pelekas, with a belvedere called The Kaiser's Throne. Glyfada has also fallen prey to development; a golf course has been constructed in the neighbourhood, and Ermones Bay, north of Glyfada (popularly held to be one on which Odysseus was washed ashore after his shipwreck, and found by Nausicaa), is equally developed.

Paxos
The smallest of the principal Ionian islands, Paxos lies ten miles south of the southernmost point of Corfu and is served by caique both from Corfu town and from the village of Kavos, which in turn is linked to Corfu town by bus. Caiques also ply between Paxos and Parga. Covered with olive trees and a few vines, mostly on the tiny dependency of Antipaxos, which produces a *rosé* wine, Paxos has one small harbour at Lakka in the north and a bigger one, protected by the islet of the Panaghia at Gaios, the capital. In rough weather it is usual to land at Lakka and take the bus to Gaios, a little pink and white amphitheatre of a town rising away from the one *plateia,* which borders the sea. The island has a bungalow-style tourist hotel just south of the capital, villas, *kaffeneions* and *tavernas.* Off the shores of Paxos, in the 3rd century BC, was fought the naval battle which

gave the domination of Corfu to the Romans; later, it is said, Antony and Cleopatra stayed here before the Battle of Actium.

Lefkas

Although technically an island, Lefkas (pop. c. 21,000) is in fact separated from the mainland only by a shallow lagoon and a narrow strait which was canalised in antiquity. It is most easily reached by a car ferry from Akarnania in Western Greece. Its centre is wild and mountainous, broken by high plateaux. Nearly all the settlements are on the eastern shore, facing the mainland across a scatter of small islets, including Scorpios, owned by the late Aristotle Onassis, and Madoura, with a lovely villa, owned by the Valaoritis family. At its northern extremity a curious, long, sandy spit with a Turko-Venetian fort on it curls towards the mainland; at the southern end is the long, sharp, whitish peninsula of Cape Doukato from which comes the island's name: Lefkas in ancient Greek means "white". From here unrequited lovers were wont to leap into the sea, following a precedent set by the poet Sappho.

History

Lefkas was colonised in ancient times by Corinth; fell to Corcyra and then to Rome. It came under the Venetians somewhat later than the other Ionians, after several periods of Turkish rule, and was next taken by the French, and then the British. Its most famous son was the 19th century Greek writer Aristoteles Valaoritis, whose statue graces the waterfront and gazes across the misty lagoon; the modern poet Sikelianos was also born here, as was the half-Irish travel writer and Japanophile, Lafcadio Hearn.

Lefkas Town

Lefkas town (pop. c. 6,500) is low-built and tightly packed, radiating in small alleys off one main street; most of the upper storeys of the houses are of wood which is more resilient to earthquake tremors than stone or brick. There are a few little baroque churches with detached Meccano-like bell towers (another precaution against earthquakes), of which the most noteworthy are Aghios Dhimitrios and Aghios Minas, both having 18th century frescoes, and the Pantokrator Cathedral, a century older, with an Italianate interior. There are hotels, including a Xenia, *kaffeneions* and *tavernas* in town and at several outlying villages.

The chief sight north of Lefkas town, by the long causeway leading to the ferry, is the ruined Sta Maura fort.

South of Lefkas Town

South of the capital there are salt-pans along the shore of Dhrepano Bay, below the site of ancient Leucas, and valleys running down from the central mountain range have small villages at their mouths. Further south again, most easily reached by caique from the town, is the deep and almost landlocked bay of Vlikho with the village of Nidri, (Mycaenean tombs) at its landward mouth. The caique passes the lonely Valaoritis villa on Madoura; on the promontory at seaward side of the bay stand the villa and tomb of the archaeologist Wilhelm Dörpfeld who spent his life trying to prove that Lefkas and not Ithaka was Odysseus's island. Completing the island circuit, Vassilikis is the prettiest village on the south coast.

Ithaka

Ithaka (pop. c. 2,500) although small and endowed with disappointingly scant remnants of the past, is nonetheless as familiar a name as any among Greek islands for its association with Odysseus. It is reached by car-ferries from Patras, calling en route at Sami on Kefallonia, and from Astakós on the Epirot mainland. It has a couple of hotels, pensions, and self-catering apartments. Almost cut in two by the huge Gulf of Molo, the island is rugged and mountainous. "No room for horses to exercise ... nor are there any meadows" said Telemachus, Odysseus's son. Cultivation is in small neatly terraced plots and consists mainly of olives, vines and some fruit and vegetables. After Odysseus's time, Ithaka figures little in history. It was ruled by Italian dynasties until the 15th century when it was sacked by the Turks. Early in the following century the Venetians repopulated it from the other Ionians. Off its shores in 1571 was fought the naval Battle of Lepanto, when the Western powers under Don John of Austria defeated the Turks.

Vathy

Vathy (meaning "deep") is the capital, theatrically situated on a deep inlet that leads out of the Gulf of Molo on the southern part of the island and thus invisible from the sea. It curls round the end of the inlet in a cluster of pastel-painted red-roofed houses that are thickest on the western side where the quay is; many are inhabited by retired seamen, for the seafaring tradition is still strong in Ithaka. There is an islet offshore from which Byron swam when he stayed here in 1823. Cheerful *kaffeneions* and *tavernas* line the waterfront, and the wine of Ithaka is justly famous.

Homeric Sites

A signpost in the village points to the stiff path to the "Nymphs' Grotto", alas indistinguishable from any other cave; beyond this again, past the village of Perakhorió, is a small plateau where Eumaios may have kept his swine, and a spring nearby has been identified with the fountain of Arethusa, where they drank. Korax, the ravens' rock, looms above; below and to the south is the only bay in this part of the island (Aghios Andreas), on which Telemachus probably landed on returning from the Peloponnese, where he went for news of his father.

The actual site of Odysseus's capital is still a subject for discussion
but it was probably at the northern end of the island, on a ridge not
far from the village of Stavros, above the west coast. It boasts a
small museum (erratic opening hours; be persistent and the key will
be found) that displays finds from the Bronze Age settlement and
from Polis, on the coast below. The ridge commands views of all the
bays in the northern part of the island. Down on Polis Bay are caves
in which fragments of bronze tripod cauldrons were found: they are
popularly held to be those which Odysseus received from the
Phaecians of Skheria (Corfu). There are several other villages at this
end of the island, which is gradually becoming developed. Frikes is
the liveliest, being a base for sailing flotillas, with plenty of *tavernas*;
Kioni is quieter. Buses and taxis link all these villages with Vathy.

Kefallonia

Kefallonia (in Greek Kefallínia; pop. c. 28,200) is separated from Ithaka
by a narrow channel. In shape it resembles a crayfish: the body is
the southern end, one "claw" stretches due north and the second
bends sideways and southwards. It is extremely mountainous and
part of the southern end is still covered with the great dark fir trees
that in antiquity were used for shipbuilding. Odysseus's ship, among
others, employed this wood. The scenery is grandiose with the
mountains creating an indented coastline, and olives and vines
growing profusely on the plateaux and in the foothills.

History
In legendary times it formed part of Odysseus's realm; during the
Classical era it was divided into four city-states and was aligned with
Athens. It was of little importance to the Romans and Byzantines but
was settled in the Middle Ages by Normans and then passed to Italian
dynasties, culminating in 300 years of Venetian rule. After this it was
taken by Napoleon's forces before coming into British hands along
with the other Ionians.

Its most famous British administrator was Sir Charles Napier, who
created the road network and the water system; he was a friend of
Byron, who stayed there in 1823 before finally making up his mind
to go Messolonghi. During World War II the occupying Italians broke
with Mussolini, sided with the Allies, and refused to take German
orders; in consequence the island was decimated by German bombers
and all but a handful of the Italians massacred by the Nazis. The
island, and in particular Argostóli, was again devastated in the 1953
earthquake.

Sami
Kefallonia has an airport that receives charter flights from Britain and
other north European countries. Independent travellers will probably
come by car ferry from Astakós, or Kyllini in the Peloponnese, or

Patras, and land at Sami. This pleasant modern little town stands at the head of a wide bay on the north coast, facing Ithaka, where Don John of Austria's fleet sheltered before Lepanto. Ancient Same, mentioned by Homer, was above the present town; remains of the walls can be seen from the waterfront.

Lake Melissani; Poros to Skala

One of Napier's roads strikes inland from Sami and across the island's mountain spine to Argostóli; off it to the north are several caves, notably that containing the vivid blue Lake Melissani (admission and boat ride 200 drachmas), which is fed by underground water channels from Argostoli bay in the southwest, some 16 kilometres (10 miles) distant. Another road off the main one twists along the mountain ridges past earthquake-shattered houses to the little new villages at the southern end of the island, notably Poros (ferries to Kyllini). This road finishes at Skala, where there are remains of an archaic temple and of a Roman building with mosaics, then joins another which winds back to Argostoli. It goes through the village of Markopoulo, whose church is invaded by mysterious though quite harmless little black snakes once a year, just before the feast of the island's patron saint, Aghios Yerasimos, on August 16th. This road also passes close to the Theotokou Sisiou monastery, perched above the sea's edge.

Argostóli

Argostóli, the capital (pop. c. 7,000; several agreeable hotels, many *kaffeneions* and *tavernas*, bus services throughout the island), is an unremarkable town architecturally, having been completely rebuilt, with much financial help from abroad, after the 1953 earthquake, but it has a beautiful situation. Overlooked by the well-preserved walls of ancient Kranoi, it sits on a shallow inlet that opens off a deep bay between the Paliki peninsula (the southern "claw" of the crayfish) and the main body of the island, and is reached by an arched, British-built causeway. The centre is Metaxas Square, named after the Greek premier who was born here. There is a small museum (open daily until mid-afternoon) with exhibits that evoke pre-1953 Argostóli. The neo-Doric lighthouse on the headland is a modern copy of the one Napier had built.

South and East of Argostóli

There is plenty to see in the neighbourhood of Argostóli. A circuit starting in a southerly direction passes the white sand beaches of Makri Yialos and Plati Yialos, with much recent tourist development. In the hills behind is a number of new little villages, many with old churches. Kourkomeláta, created by the shipowning Vergotis family, almost resembles a Californian suburb. Kefallonia is noted for its ship-owners, its doctors and its professors; among the latter, the great 20th-century archaeologist, the late Spiridon Marinatos. Above Kourkomeláta, is Metaxáta, where a plaque commemorates Byron's sojourn; nearby have been found Classical-period tombs. Higher up,

Western Greece and the Ionian Islands

Mazarakáta is the site of an important Mycaenean necropolis and, overlooking them all, are the imposing remains of the mediaeval capital of the island, huddled around the castle of Aghios Georgios and abandoned for Argostóli in the mid-18th century. Further up still in the hills, in the valley of Omala, is the convent of Aghios Gerasimos, founded in 1554 by a hermit venerated for casting out demons. His mummy is kept there, in a silver sarcophagus, and paraded on his August feast day and on October 20th every year, when the mentally afflicted prostrate themselves in its path.

Lixouri
Lixouri is the second largest town on Kefallonia, isolated on the Paliki peninsula by poor roads, though connected to the capital opposite it by a car ferry across the bay which passes "Napier's lighthouse" and the now disused sea-mills built in the early days of the British Protectorate across the races that feed the underground channels to Lake Melissani. It is a low, white, modern town, pleasant but undistinguished, with a shady *plateia* surrounded by trees.

Northern Kefallonia
In the extreme north of the island is Fiskardo, reached by a steeply pitched road (another of Napier's) which passes en route the incomparably-set village of Assos. Although modern, Assos is a ravishing sight, lying across a narrow isthmus that separates two bays edged with cliffs. At the end of the isthmus, a Venetian castle with massive walls crowns a little promontory.

Fiskardo, named after the Norman warrior Robert Guiscard, conqueror of much of Southern Italy, who died here of the plague in 1085, is the only village on Kefallonia that was not destroyed by the 1953 earthquake. Around the waterfront are well-proportioned pale stone houses, some dating back to Venetian days; yachts bob against the broad quayside fringed with acacias and orange trees, and small boats wait to ferry people to and from local beaches. As a resort, it is considerably livelier than Assos, with many *tavernas* and boutiques.

Zakinthos

Zakinthos or Zante (pop. c. 30,000) lies some 16 kilometres (10 miles) south of Kefallonia, opposite the great castle of Hlemoutsi on the west coast of the Peloponnese. It has an airport that takes foreign charter flights as well as local ones to Athens, and is also reached by car ferry (several times daily) from Killini in the Peloponnese. It is bisected by a central spine of mountains running north-north west to south-south east; on the west coast they drop steeply into the sea and there is little habitation. The eastern half of the island, however, is exceptionally beautiful and fertile: its praises have been sung since ancient times. It is rich in currant-vines and olives, and in springtime is covered thickly with the wild flowers that earned it its Venetian nickname of "flor di Levante".

Zakinthos is mentioned by Homer, and appears to have been populous and active in the ancient world down to the Roman era, since when its history followed much the same lines as those of the other Ionians. It, too, knew nearly 300 years of Venetian rule, and it was part of the British Protectorate for half a century thereafter.

Zakinthos Town

The capital, Zakinthos, has several good hotels, numerous *tavernas* and *kaffeneions*. It lies along a gentle bay on the east coast, stretching for well over a mile from end to end but not extending far inland. During the Venetian era it was busy and important as well as being exceptionally beautiful: little baroque *palazzi* flanked the waterfront and lined the main street and there was a fine opera house (Zakinthos was, and still is, strongly musical). But the 1953 earthquake caused more devastation here even than in the other Ionians, and in a matter of minutes the town was reduced to rubble. It was, however, rebuilt more lovingly than Argostóli, and as a result there are echoes of its Venetian glory in the arcades around Solomos Square and along the main street; although of concrete, they are white-painted and harmonious.

Solomos Square, named after the Greek national poet who was a native of Zakinthos, yawns widely away from the waterfront; off it runs the long mole against which even quite large ships can moor. Close to the junction of square and mole is the church of Aghios Nikolaos tou Molou, dating from the 16th century: enough remained after the earthquake for it to have been well reconstructed. The square, neatly planted with orange trees, is dominated by a statue of Solomos, behind which is the small museum (open daily, except Tuesdays, until mid-afternoon). It contains carved Byzantine altar screens and paintings rescued from destroyed churches, and some good post-Byzantine ikons. On the site of Solomos's house is another small museum (open at the same hours; entrance free) devoted to mementoes of the poet and other eminent Zakinthiots; it stands in a small square behind Solomos Square. Above and inland of the town the former Venetian *kastro* rises on a flat-topped hill from which the views are staggering.

At the southern end of the town are two more notable churches: the Panaghia Faneroméni, with a free standing belfry, all rebuilt as far as possible on the same fine lines as before its destruction, and Aghios Dionysios (frescoes) which was not affected by the 1953 earthquake. St Dionysios is the island's patron saint, and principally concerned with the welfare of fishermen; his remains repose in a silver casket that is paraded around the town on August 24th each year.

Zakinthos to Cape Yerakos

South of Zakinthos a good road runs between Mount Scopus and the sea. At Arghasi, 3 kilometres (2 miles) from town, there is a narrow

Western Greece and the Ionian Islands

beach with several hotels, apartment houses and other tourist facilities. The road goes through Vasilikó, a straggling village with *tavernas* and inns, and ends in a track that leads down to peaceful little Porto Roma, so called because one of the island's great Venetian families used to moor their boat here. There is a fine beach and beyond is Cape Yerakas.

Laganas Bay

The huge bay of Laganas, enclosing a few islets, occupies the entire south-west coast of the island from Cape Yerakas to Cape Marathias. Long gently shelving and mainly sandy, it is beginning to witness some large-scale development. The scattered and rather haphazard small inns and *tavernas* that previously occupied it were not picturesque enough for the new-style building to cause much regret; what is far more regrettable is the threat the new development poses for loggerhead turtles who come ashore at the adjacent "Crystal Bay" to lay their eggs. Speedboats, motor cycles and cars, and even curious pedestrians with torches and loud voices, all represent a hazard to these sensitive and fast-disappearing creatures, for which the efforts of both Greek and foreign conservationists may have come too late. At the far end of the road that skirts Laganas is Keri, above a smaller bay; close to it, on the edge of a patch of marsh, are the darkly oozing bitumen springs, mentioned by the ancient historians, that were — and still are — used for caulking boats.

Central Plain

Inland from the road between Keri and Zakinthos lies the fertile central plain of the island, once divided among a handful of feudal ruling Venetian families but now split into smallholdings and dotted with cottages and hamlets. One of these, Makhairado, boasts the finest village church on the island with an ornate interior graced by excellent carvings.

North of Zakinthos

North of Zakinthos the road leaves town by way of the British cemetery; crumbling now, but evocative of the years when the ties between Britain and the island were strong. It goes past the village of Pokhali and the little plateau of Strani, between the *kastro* and the hill of Akrotiri at the end of the headland, where Solomos liked to sit and meditate, and then runs inland along a broad shallow valley full of currant vines. A road to the right runs down to the popular beach of Tsilívi; another road, just inland, runs parallel to it. Both join at the village of Katastari at the north end of the valley and down to the coast at the sheltered resort of Alikiés where there are salt pans and an excellent beach. Continuing north, there are fantastic views as you climb away from the coast, reaching as far as the castle of Hlemoutsi on the mainland. A brief detour to the west takes in the Anafonítria convent, with a medieval tower; the main road ends at the sizeable hill-village of Volímes, where rag-rugs and crochet items are made.

Kithira

Kithira (pop. c. 3,500) last of the Ionians and historically the seventh of the group, is, geographically speaking, an appendage of the southern Peloponnese, lying at the mouth of the Gulf of Lakonia. It has an airport, with seasonal services to Athens, and is also served by boat from Neapolis and hydrofoils from Piraeus. It is covered with low, rocky hills, largely uncultivated, and has a wild remote atmosphere about it.

History
Its history is a long though largely unknown one: at one time it was a centre for the worship of the Syrian Aphrodite and it was certainly a Minoan colony in about 2000 BC: the excavation in 1964 of a Minoan trading post, dating from that time or slightly later, first led me to visit the island, which is now beginning to develop a fairly low-profile tourist industry. Kithira played a part in the Peloponnesian War, endured many an invasion during the Middle Ages, and finally came under Venice, along with the other Ionians, in 1717. Since World War II, when its inhabitants bravely assisted many British troops to escape from the German-occupied mainland, it has been greatly depopulated by emigration to Australia but, as a result of this link, many of the inhabitants speak English.

Kithiran Villages
Ferries call at both Aghia Pelaghia, a tiny village (rooms to let, pensions) with a colourful boatyard at the northern end of the island, and then at Kapsali (inn, *tavernas*, self-catering apartments), a small port on an exquisite double-headed bay in the south. Khora, the chief township, stands on a high rocky terrace above Kapsali, with a mediaeval *kastro* at its vanishing point. There is a simple inn, and beds may be rented in private houses. The small Minoan site at Kastri overlooks the eastern shore, near Avlémonas; it can be visited without charge upon request at the nearby farmhouse. Among other interesting spots are the pretty, well-watered village of Milopótamos in the west; the site of ancient Kithira on Mt Paliokastro in the southeast; Paliochora, with a ruined Byzantine fort, inland of Aghia Pelaghia in the north; and several caves. But the chief appeal of the island is its simplicity and other-worldliness. Tiny Antikythira, off its south coast, with only two hamlets and fragmentary ruins, is more isolated still.

Minoan Palace of Phaistos

Crete

Two hundred and fifty-six kilometres (160 miles) long and fifty-eight kilometres (36 miles) wide, the island (pop. c. 503,000) is bisected geographically by a mountain spine that runs its entire length from the White Mountains in the west through the central Ida massif to the Diktaian and Thripte mountains in the east. There are high plateaux in each of the three main ranges; otherwise cultivation and population are largely confined to the northern coastal strip and the central Mesara plain in the south. The south coast, with the exception of Mesara and the lerápetra area in the east, is precipitous and rugged.

Climatically temperate, and also highly fertile, it is intensely cultivated with vines, olives, carobs, fruit and vegetables. It has a huge variety of wild flowers, many of them unique to the island, and some mountain wild life (ibex, wild cat).

History

Largest of Greece's islands, Crete is in many respects the most un-Greek, with an historical and cultural background that differs enough from that of other regions to have given it a strongly individual personality. Its size and strategic position in the Eastern Mediterranean, lying midway between North Africa, Anatolia and the Greek mainland, are largely responsible for this.

Minoan Periods

Its earliest inhabitants (about 6000 BC) were probably Earth-goddess worshippers from the East and over the next three millennia establish-ed themselves is such places as Knossos and Phaistos where, with the dawn of the Bronze Age, they gradually developed highly civilised communities. For nearly 2,000 years, in three distinct phases, the civili-sation, named Minoan after the legendary King Minos (son of Europa, and Zeus in the guise of a bull), flourished throughout the island.

The first phase was the Pre-Palace or Early Minoan. The Old Palace, or Middle Minoan, period (from about 1950 BC), saw the building of the earliest palaces (such as Mallia) and cities, all of which were largely destroyed by earthquake some two hundred years later. The third and last stage, Late Minoan (New Palace), beginning about 1700 BC, witnessed the rebuilding of the palaces on a far more sophisticated scale, and their decoration with eleborate frescoes.

Plumbing and drainage systems were well developed and the prosper-ity of this period is evident from the large areas of storage jars *(pithoi)* full of grain, oil, etc., that have been found in the palaces. There is much evidence, too, of maritime trade with Egypt and the Middle East, and Cretan ships must also have protected the island since strong shore fortifications are absent. Systems of syllabic writing were used and the mother-goddess continued to be worshipped.

The destruction of this civilisation around 1450 BC was until quite recently attributed to earthquakes, fires and tidal waves following the volcanic eruption on Thera, or Santorini. Recent excavations, how-ever, suggest that local wars between the palace-cities had weakened most of them for many generations, after which Knossos emerged as the strongest power. It is also suggested that Knossos was eventually sacked by the Mycaeneans in 1450 BC, rather than having been destroy-ed by natural causes and reoccupied later by Mycaeneans. In any case, finds from such religious sites as the Diktaian and Ida caves testify to a continuous, and artistically increasingly developed, culture from that point onwards.

Greeks, Romans, Saracens

During the Classical and Hellenistic periods from the 5th century BC Crete, like the mainland, was made up of small autonomous city states. They took no part in the Persian or mainland wars, however, and escaped the Macedonian conquest, but after the Roman conquest in 67 BC Gortyn, in Southern Crete, became the capital of the province of Cyrenaica. The island continued prosperous in early Byzantine times until overrun by Saracens in the early 8th century and occupied for nearly 150 years.

Venetians, Turks, Modern Greece

From the 13th to the 17th centuries Crete was ruled first by the

Genoese and then, for over 400 years, by the Venetians. Its period of Turkish occupation was short by comparison with the mainland, lasting only 230 years, but it was a time of neglect and great poverty. Crete was not united with Greece until 1913. In World War II, the Battle of Crete (May, 1941) was one of the bitterest in the island's history and ended with the evacuation of British and Commonwealth troops from the southern port of Khora Sfakíon.

Iraklion

Iraklion (pop. c. 101,500) is the chief commercial city and also the main tourist centre by virtue of its central position and good communications: there is an international airport, car ferries to Piraeus, buses for all parts of the north coast. Since earliest times the harbour for Knossos, it was made the capital (under the name of Candia) by the Venetians. It was, however, largely destroyed by the Turks and little remains of its Venetian period apart from the inner harbour and its fortress, the completely restored Venetian Loggia and St Mark's Hall in the main street (25th August Street), the lovely 17th century Morosini Fountain opposite St Mark's Hall, and parts of the city wall and gates. Otherwise the town is modern and, although lively, not very interesting. It is a good shopping centre (25th August Street and Vassilisis Konstantinou) with a colourful food market (1866 Street) that also boasts numerous good little *tavernas,* has a good range of hotels in all classes, and is a convenient excursion centre with organised tours to all parts of the island.

Museum

Its glory, of course is its Archaeological Museum (open daily, except Mondays, all day long). The exhibits relate to the many excavated sites on the island. Here are the finds from all periods of Cretan history from the Neolithic and Pre-Palace periods to the Roman, of which the pottery, statuary, jewellery, seals, weapons and fragmentary frescoes from the Late Minoan period are the most sensational objects. A rich museum, despite its relatively small size, and beautifully arranged, it repays many visits.

Knossos

The principal sight in the environs of Iraklion is Knossos (open daily, all day long), some four miles inland, past the remains of the Roman Villa Dionysos. Almost continuously occupied throughout Crete's ancient history, most of the visible remains of Knossos are from the later 1600 BC Minoan (New Palace) era, much restored by the site's first excavator, Sir Arthur Evans. Opinion is still sharply divided over the wisdom and merit of such extensive reconstruction, which includes re-created frescoes and rebuilt painted pillars. But the average traveller, once he has absorbed the initial shock and adjusted to it, is probably grateful for its assistance in deciphering the bewilderingly labyrinthine ruins, much of whose structure was originally of wood and consequently totally destroyed.

This is, of course, the site of the original "labyrinth" legendarily designed by Daedelus to house the monstrous Minotaur, offspring of a
bull and Minos's wife, Pasiphae (who had concealed herself in an
imitation heifer also made by Daedelus). The monster, who annually
devoured seven youths and seven maidens of Athens (Minos's re-
venge upon the city for the slaying of his son), was eventually killed
by Theseus, prince of Athens, with the help of Minos's daughter
Ariadne. Daedelus, forced to flee for his part in this deed, made wings
both for himself and his son Icarus and they took to the air. But
Icarus flew too high, and the sun melted the wax in his wings, so
that he fell into the Aegean on the spot now known as the island of
Ikaria.

Southern Crete

Mesara Plain, Kamares Cave
From Knossos it is possible to cross to the south of Crete via the
wine-village of Arkhanes, in whose neighbourhood other Minoan sites
have been excavated. Notable is the one signposted Vathýpetro, some
4 kilometres (2½ miles) to the south: a late Minoan villa, with staggering views. The Mesara plain, however, is more usually reached
by the main road, south from Iraklion, winding through the lovely
fertile foothills of Mount Ida. A side road, from Aghia Varvara, leads
to the important 14th-century churches of the Vrondisi Monastery
and Valsamonero; also to Kamares, where mules can be hired for
the climb to the Kamares cave, where there have been notable pottery
finds, and the summit of Mount Ida beyond.

Phaistos; Aghia Triadha, Gortyn
The great palace-site of Phaistos stands on a low levelled-off hilltop
commanding magnificent views of the plain. Excavated by the French,
its ruins are both smaller and simpler than those of Knossos, dating
mostly from the Late Minoan period; among its most interesting
features are the enormous Grand Staircase and the Royal Apartments
on the northern side of the site. There is a Tourist Pavilion on an
adjacent low hill where meals and refreshments are available. The
site is open daily, all day long. The other important Minoan site in
this area is Aghia Triadha (the name is that of the Venetian church
close by) which is open daily until mid-afternoon. The big, impressive
villa, or small palace, from the Late Minoan age, with the ruins of a
settlement around it, is only minutes by road from Phaistos.

Gortyn
Also close by is Gortyn (Gortís) (open daily, all day) dating back to
the 7th century BC, which later became the Roman capital of the
province. Its ruins include a theatre, an odeon, a basilica and a wall
behind the odeon inscribed with the Laws of Gortyn in about 480 BC.

Crete

Aghia Galini and Lenta

After Phaistos the road branches, one arm leading down to Mátala where the ancient rock tombs in the sea cliffs were at one time popular with the hippies; now the village has expanded greatly in the interests of more remunerative tourism. The other road goes through Timbáki to the steeply-sloping seaside resort of Aghia Galini, also experiencing a tourist boom. Thereafter it turns inland, through the village of Spili, and crosses to Rethymnon on the north coast. After Spili there is a turn-off along a poor road to the dramatically situated Prevéli monastery on a magnificent gorge overlooking the south coast. Returning to Iraklion, another side road, between Phaistos and Gortyn, leads south through the mountains to the large and isolated Hellenistic-Roman Asclepeion site of Lenta, perched on a wild hillside.

Eastern Crete

To Mallia

East of Iraklion a new highway runs along the north shore past the Tourist Office beach and new beach hotels, past the airport to Amnisos where there are Minoan and Archaic remains, and from where Idomeneos is said to have sailed for the Trojan War. It continues through a string of resorts that virtually shade into one another and the ancient site of Hersoníssos, to the great seaside palace site of Mallia, and then turns inland. Alongside the palace site is a rapidly growing resort with many new hotels and *tavernas.*

Selenari Pass, Elounda, Spinalonga

Soon the highway runs into a tunnel and the old road twists up the dramatic Selenari Pass to a little church and shrine in the village, where pre-tunnel travellers would pause for spiritual refreshments as well as a drink from the roadside spring. At Neapolis there is a choice of detours. The first is past the site of the archaic city of Dreros to Elounda, a lively resort with mainly high-class hotels that has sprung from nothing in barely two decades. Offshore, the ancient city of Olous lies submerged and beyond it is the Venetian-fortified island of Spinalonga, once a leper colony, now uninhabited. This road continues parallel with the shore to the sprawling outskirts of Aghios Nikólaos.

Lassithi Plateau, Diktaean Cave

The other detour is to the Lassithi Plateau (also reachable from Hersonissos). Both fine scenic roads lead to the high, mountain-encircled plain where windmills flail the air from fields of vegetables and orchards. Several little villages are scattered about the plateau and several ancient sites as well, the most notable being the Diktaean Cave near Psykhro. Here Zeus was born of the Earth-goddess Rhea who concealed him in the cave to protect him from his father, Kronos, whom he was destined to usurp.

Aghios Nikólaos

Aghios Nikólaos, with its many hotels, restaurants and tourist shops, is peerlessly sited on the great Gulf of Mirabello around a deep, still inner harbour edged to landward by sheer cliffs. The white town sprawls behind it, and along an irregular waterfront that stretches away from the outer harbour. Its very picturesqueness has spelt its doom, for it has been grossly over-developed and is now crowded and noisy and as much an international resort as a Cretan one. It is, however, a convenient base for Eastern Crete.

Kritsa; Lato; Gournia

In the hills immediately behind it is the big hill village of Kritsa (also much manicured and commercialised, thanks to increasing tourism) where rugs are woven and where, in a field, is the tiny 14th century frescoed church of the Panaghia Kera, one of the most vivid in the island. Above this again is the site of the Archaic Greek city of Lato, or Goulás, high in a lonely saddle between two hills; scant remains but stupendous views.

South-east of Aghios Nikólaos, the shores of the Gulf are gradually being developed with hotels, villas, and the new resort of Istron. Beyond, on a gentle hillside, are the Late Minoan ruins of the city of Gournia. Excavated by the Americans this site, with its little streets of houses crowned by a small palace, is open daily until mid-afternoon and rewarding to explore.

South to Ierápetra

Beyond it the road forks right across the narrowest neck of the island for Ierápetra (pop. c. 8,500), a fishing village and fast-growing resort strung along a broad beach on the south coast. There are a few Roman ruins, a Turkish minaret and fountain, and a house where Napoleon is supposed to have stayed en route to Egypt in 1798. Good new roads lead east and west out of Ierápetra; to the east, the depopulated old village of Koutsounari has been restored; houses can be rented. Past it are several beachside inns and *tavernas* as far as Makriyialos, a developing small resort where the new road turns inland and north for Sitia. West of Ierápetra, the coastal plain is heavily cultivated with fruit and vegetables growing beneath green polythene tunnels that dominate every view. Some 20 kilometres (12 miles) from Ierápetra, just off the road, is the early Minoan site of Myrtos, and beyond it another side road leads down to the isolated monastery and tiny coastal hamlet of Arvi (inns and *tavernas),* over-looked by a monastery. The main road continues as far as Ano Vianos, a hill village from where it is possibe to weave back inland through wonderful scenery to Iraklion.

Sitia

Back on the north coast, instead of forking right past Gournia you can continue east across the hills above the Gulf of Mirabello. There are beautiful views looking to the rear, and a side road to the Early Minoan site of Mokhlos. The road rejoins the shore at Sitia (pop. c. 6,500), terraced up a steep hill, with a shady waterfront and a long sandy beach beyond it. Were it nearer to an airport, Sitia would doubtless already be densely developed, but this is only happening gradually. There are *tavernas* on the waterfront, a few inns and one fair-sized hotel on the beach, and scattered villa developments further east.

Still further east, in wild and remote upland country overlooking the sea, is the enclosed — almost fortified — monastery of Toploú, with a fine 18th century ikon guarded by two monks and several dogs. Some eight miles further, at the north-eastern tip of the island, is the unexpectedly palm-edged beach of Vai, with a distinct North African flavour, and the ancient site of Itanos.

Palaikastro and Kato Zakros
From here one can come back to the main road at Palaikastro, a Late Minoan settlement on the edge of an olive grove above the sea, and continue over the final mountain ridge, a lonely and dramatic drive, to Kato Zakros. At the foot of the gorge is the important Late Minoan harbour site of Zakro, open daily all day. On the seaward edge of the little plain that now separates it from the sea is a hamlet with rooms to let, *tavernas* and good pebble beach.

Western Crete
Three routes to the West
Starting again from Iraklion, bound for Western Crete, there are three possible routes. The newest is the National Road bordering the sea, passing behind several tourist hotels and below the village of Fodele, vigorously exploiting its tenuous claim to be the birthplace of El Greco (Domenikos Theotokópoulos). The older main road runs inland of it through pleasant hill scenery with turnings for Melidhone (a cave where a band of Cretans was smoked to death by the Turks in 1824), Eleftherna, with the ruins of an ancient Greek city above it, and the Arkhádiou Monastery. Open daily in the mornings and from 1500 until 1700, it is a handsome ensemble of buildings in a beautiful situation, and is renowned for its particularly heroic resistance to a Turkish siege in 1866.

The third route winds further inland still, to Tylissos, where three interesting Late Minoan villas, or sizeable country houses, stand at the top of the village. The precisely-excavated ruins, open daily until early afternoon, demonstrate that labyrinthine layout was not the hallmark just of palaces, and on this smaller scale is more easily comprehensible. Over a pass to the west is Anoghia, a weavers' village rebuilt after destruction by the Germans in World War II. From here one can climb Mount Ida in about five hours (there is a car track too) to the Idaian Cave, another contender for the title of Zeus's birthplace; it is open in the summer season except when excavations are in progress. One more sharp turning to the left before Réthymno leads up to the high, beautiful Amari Valley and the Assómato Monastery whose church has early 13th-century frescoes and older mosaics.

Réthymno
Réthymno, a Venetian-walled town (pop. c. 18,000), although greatly grown in recent years, still has some fine old houses and many traces of Turkish occupation, including several minarets and a fountain. Its museum, and the Venetian fort, or *frourio*, that dominates the harbour, are open daily, except Tuesdays, until mid-afternoon. There are lively fish *tavernas* along the harbour and the town is the venue for the Cretan Wine Festival at the end of July. To either side of the town stretch long, sandy beaches that are being heavily built up with hotels and apartments; town hotels include a Xenia.

West of Réthymno
From Réthymno, the new National Road parallels the coast and then cuts inland across the base of the headland that ends in Cape Drápano. A turnoff, signposted to Kalami and Kalives, passes beneath a huge Turkish fort, now a prison, looming above Kalami, and continues through the still-unspoiled seaside villages of Kalives and Almirida. Just before Almirida on the left are the remains of a Byzantine church of the 13th century, with attractive mosaics on the floor; it is fenced off from the road but a convenient gap in the fence allows access.

Sfakia and the Southwest Coast
The old road, just inland of the new one, goes through Vrisses, a shady village watered by springs and a popular stopping-place for motorists and excursion coaches; the yoghurt produced there is particularly delicious. From Vrisses a dramatic road over the shoulder of the White Mountains crosses the island to Sfakia (Khora Sfakion, or 'place of the Sfakiots') on the rugged southwest coast. This tiny port with its simple inn and a handful of pensions saw the evacuation of many hundreds of British and Commonwealth troops during World War II. On a sand-edged promontory to the east of it is the angular bulk of the 14th-century Venetian Frangokástello, said to be haunted in early May by the ghosts of Cretan revolutionaries who died during a Turkish siege in 1828. A patchy road leads on past it eastwards to Selia and eventually back to Réthymno, and another leads west to the isolated hill village of Anopolis.

Beyond this, the coast is too precipitous for roads, but there is a boat link from Sfakia to the village of Aghia Roumeli (via Loutra) to the west, where the Samarian Gorge reaches the sea (see below). Boats can also be hired to take you on to Souyia, a tiny seaside village with an early Byzantine mosaic in its church. The hamlet of Rodhovani, with frescoed churches, is in the hills above it. Paleokhora,

Crete

a big village with a fine beach and and the remains of a Venetian fort, is the last port of call along this coast; it has inns and *tavernas* and is connected by a good mountain road with the north shore.

Aptera; Soudha; Akrotiri
The main north coast highway rejoins the seashore after the Kalami/ Kalives turnoff, shortly after which another turning, to the left, leads within a few kilometres to a fork. One branch goes up to another former Turkish fort, the twin of the Kalami one but disused, from which there are wide views; the other leads to the site of ancient Aptera. Open day-long every day except on Mondays and Thursday mornings, its chief sight is a huge and magnificent triple-vaulted Roman cistern built into the side of the hill; again, the views are tremendous.

After Aptera, the main road skirts Soudha Bay (naval base, photograhy forbidden) and from it a side road leads through Soudha itself to the beautifully kept Military Cemetery at the head of the bay, where hundreds of British and Commonwealth World War II combatants lie buried. Further north on the Akrotiri peninsula that half-encloses Soudha Bay (and where the airport is) the tomb of the statesman Eleftherios Venizelos lies on a landscaped hilltop — from the terrace one gets a bird's eye view of Khaniá; nearby are a couple of *tavernas* patronised by cheerful family parties come to pay their respects to the man who campaigned for Crete's reunion with Greece. At the peninsula's tip, Stavros is a messy clutter of summer shacks around a lovely bay. Kalathas, closer to Khaniá, is more attractive and has good *tavernas*. The Akrotiri peninsula is a favourite residential area for wealthy Khaniots and three monasteries are sited among its hills.

Khaniá
Capital of Crete (pop. c. 47,500) and the site of ancient Kydonia, Khaniá is a handsome town with shady squares and some beautiful Venetian houses at its heart. It is connected by air with Athens and by sea (from Soudha) with Piraeus, as well as being the terminal for bus services throughout Western Crete. Among its major landmarks are a magnificent covered market; the remains of Venetian walls; a huge former Venetian arsenal (as yet unrestored); two linked harbours and, between them, a former mosque that now houses the Tourist Office. It has a number of good hotels and waterfront restaurants (the ones around the westernmost, or outer, harbour being the most touristy and expensive); masses of good shops and a cobweb of narrow, attractive old streets. Khania's newly-reorganised museum is housed in a disused church in Khalidon Street, which runs down to the outer harbour, and is open daily, except Tuesdays, all day. It houses fine painted-clay larnaces (burial-vessels) from the Minoan period as well as other finds from various sites in the western half of the island, all well-displayed and labelled.

Samaria Gorge

The main inland excursion from Khaniá is to Omalos for the walk through the Samaria Gorge. This has become a *de rigueur* organised mass outing for up to 3,000 people a day in the summer season, starting before dawn from their resorts and returning after dusk. Europe's longest true gorge, it extends for 18 kilometres (just over 11 miles) and the tour organisers allow four to six hours to cover the distance. At the end, boats take walkers from Aghia Roumeli to rejoin their coaches at Sfakia, which allows time for most people to have a swim and a meal at one of the many Aghia Roumeli *tavernas* before starting the return trip. In the less-crowded season it is possible to appreciate the dramatic beauty of the gorge even on a group excursion; independent travellers might consider starting much later in the day and spending the night at Aghia Roumeli (it is no longer permitted to camp at the deserted village of Samaria, halfway down the gorge, where there are rest-rooms), and either arranging to be met at Sfakia the following day or doing the walk in reverse, uphill and against the human tide, for which more time should be allowed. The walk is not difficult; proper shoes should be worn but climbing boots are unnecessary and as one is often close to the course of the stream, water need not be taken. For those who cannot face the entire distance, 'lazy' excursions are arranged, by boat each way from Sfakia to Aghia Roumeli with enough time to walk part-way up the lower end of the gorge — at least as far as the so-called 'Iron Gates' where the cliffs are mere metres apart.

Laki and Meskla

An even less taxing inland excursion from Khaniá is by car along the Omalos road as far as Laki and then left up the Keritis valley to Meskla, at the upper edge of which is a fine small Byzantine church. A poor but perfectly passable road winds on above Meskla through beautiful mountain scenery and comes down again to Thériso, a charming village at the head of another gorge — this time with a good road through it that eventually leads back to Khaniá.

West of Khania

West of the capital, the main road hugs the shoreline which is now almost solid with tourist development from the outskirts of Khaniá through Aghia Marina, Platanias and Maleme, this latter the site of an airfield that saw some fierce fighting during the Battle of Crete in May 1941. After the turnoff to Paleokhora the development thins; Kolimvari, at the base of the Rhodopos peninsula and overlooked by the huge Goniás Monastery, is charming. Further west is the Bay of Kisamou with Kastelli-Kisamou (often, confusingly, signposted Kisamos) at its centre. An unprepossessing little town despite a good beach and harbour (ferries to Kythira and the Peloponnese) it stands on the site of ancient Kisamos, the port of Polirínia in the hills above, where a stiffish walk up through the half-deserted village brings you to the scanty ancient remains — notably the base of a temple of

Artemis that now shores up a small church and cemetery.

Westwards again, across the base of Cape Vouha, the road winds across beautiful low hills to Platanos, doubles back on itself and descends to huge empty beaches edged by cliffs and the site of ancient Falásarna, originally a well-walled port. However the land has risen by eight metres or more since its time, and all that can be seen today, once the straggle of small pensions and *tavernas* is passed, is stretches of massive walling half-encircling a rocky outcrop and a solitary rock-cut throne beside the track. But it is a wild and dramatically lovely spot.

The House of Cleopatra, Dilos

Central Aegean Islands

The Cyclades

Between the southernmost tip of Evia and the north coast of Crete, between Cape Sounion in the west and Ikaria and Astypalaia in the east, the surface of the Aegean is broken in hundreds of places by the rocky peaks of a mountainous sunken plateau, collectively and somewhat loosely called the Cyclades (pronounced Kikládes) although technically many of the islands belong to the Sporades. Rugged and virtually treeless, the vast majority are without water and therefore uninhabited, but a score or so are cultivated, mainly with vines and olives, and support life; and a visit to one or more of them is an essential part of the Greek experience.

Climatically they are equable: what little rain they get falls largely in the months of December, January and February. The air is exceptionally clear and soft and, in the summer months, the heat is tempered by a north wind: the *meltemi*. This blows gustily throughout July, August and early September and anyone prone to seasickness should be wary of it.

The Central Aegean Islands

How to get there
All the Cyclades are linked by regular shipping or hydrofoil services to Piraeus, but different ships call at different groups of islands and an itinerary should therefore not be planned without consulting the domestic sea schedules. Rough routings of the more popular ones are: Kithnos, Serifos, Sifnos, Milos; Siros, Paros, Naxos, Ios; Naxos, Ios, Thera (Santorini), Iraklion; Tinos, Mikonos, Paros, Ios, Thera. Mikonos is also included on some routes to the Dodecanese, and Thera (Santorini) en route from Piraeus to Eastern Crete and the Dodecanese or from Thessaloníki to Iraklion. There are also two routes from Rafina; to Syros, Paros and Naxos, and to Andros, Tinos and Mikonos. Regular short cruises almost invariably call at both Mikonos and Santorini/Thera.

History
In earliest times the islands' Cycladic, (pronounced Kikladic) civilisation roughly paralleled the Minoan on Crete: most of the islands were under Minoan domination until the Mycaeneans eclipsed them. As Mycaenean power waned in its turn, the islands were occupied by the Ionians, who made Delos their religious focal point and formed the Delian League. During the Persian wars they suffered various invasions, the majority aligning themselves in the interim periods with Athens, and eventually most fell to Macedon during the 4th century BC. After a brief servitude to Rhodes in the 2nd century BC, it was the turn of Rome and they remained Roman until the foundation of the Byzantine Empire. Thereafter they were more or less prey for successive invaders until the early 13th century, when the Venetians parcelled them out among various powerful families, some of whom continued to rule their fiefs even after the Turks overran Greece. The Ottoman Empire was not, however, particularly interested in the islands and, apart from occasional depradations by visitors from Western Europe in search of antiquities, and the unhappy period in the 18th century when they constituted the battleground for the Russian-Turkish war, they were left in peace until Greece declared its independence of Turkey in 1821 and the Cyclades returned to their mother country.

Andros

Andros (pop. c. 9,000) is one of the largest and best-wooded of the Cyclades, more topographically akin to nearby Evia than to the more southerly islands. It is most conveniently visited from the port of Rafina in Attica; it is popular with Athenians but has so far not been over-developed for foreign tourists. Although sacred to Dionysos in ancient times, it has no important ruins from those eras; Venetian remains predominate.

The principal port is Gavrion (hotels). Also on the west coast near it is Batsi, the main beach resort, with numerous holiday villas, inns, small hotels and *tavernas*. A bus service runs from Batsi across the centre of the island, which is punctuated by unusually-constructed stone walls and mediaeval dovecotes, to Andros town above the east coast, where there are several more hotels. En route are Palaiópolis, site of the ancient city, and the old hill villages of Ménites and Mesariá (church). The whitewashed island capital, flanking a marble-paved main street, stretches along a pretty promonotry between two bays, providing good swimming, to a crumbling Venetian fortress at its tip.

Kea

Kea (pop. c. 1,700) closest of all the Cyclades to Athens is only lightly developed with the building of villas, apartments and beach hotels (at Korissía and Koundouros). It is relatively fertile and was well populated in antiquity, supporting four city-states. This era has yielded some important archaeological finds at Vourkári, notably an archaic *kouros* statue now in the National Museum in Athens, Cycladic and Helladic pottery and clay figures. The main port is white-painted Korissía on a bay in the north-west (served by boats from Lavrion) with the ruins nearby of ancient Korissía and of an even earlier site. A road leads north from it to the Panaghia Kastriani monastery, passing several good beaches and the archaeological excavations at Aghia Irini.

The capital, Khora, is inland and above Korissía to the south-east, the two being connected by a bus service. It is dominated by an acropolis where a Venetian *kastro*, now largely destroyed, stood on the site of a temple of Apollo. There is also a small museum. Outside the town the huge rough rock-carving of a lion is worth seeing; so too is the ruined Aghia Marina Convent, built against a big square Hellenic stone tower to the south, en route to the ruins of another ancient city called Poiessa and to the Koundouros summer beach hotels at the southern end of the island.

Tinos

Tinos (pop. c. 8,000), whose northernmost tip almost touches Andros and reached from Rafina as well as Piraeus, is one of the more touristically developed islands, with a popular large beach hotel about a mile west of the capital, plus many lesser ones. It is both an Orthodox place of pilgrimage and a stronghold of the Roman Catholic faith. The town itself is sizeable by island standards, a packed cluster of white cubes grouped along and behind a busy waterfront lined with *kaffeneions* and *tavernas*. Its focal point, at the top of the main street, is the white marble Panaghia Evangelistria church which houses a miraculous curative ikon of the Holy Virgin, venerated throughout Greece, around which centre the important festivals of August 15th and March 25th. The August 15th celebrations in 1940 were shattered by the torpedoing of a Greek naval vessel in Tinos harbour. There is an archaeological museum (open daily, except Tuesdays, until mid-afternoon) and masses of souvenir shops. Outside the town, to the west, are the foundations of a Sanctuary of Poseidon, who is said to have saved Tinos from a plague of serpents by sending storks to consume them.

The centre of the island is carefully cultivated, Tinos wine being especially renowned, and punctuated by little white villages and square Venetian dovecotes similar to those on Andros. The ruins of the ancient capital lie inland, below the Xomvourgo *kastro* (steep climb, fabulous view). There are bus services from the quayside to most of these places, and a number of good beaches are also accessible from them, notably Ormos Panourmou below the big village of Panormos in the north, and Aghios Nikitas, below Isternia.

Kithnos

Lying just south of Kea, Kithnos (pop. c. 1,500), reached from Lavrion as well as Piraeus, is still largely undeveloped. Its small population lives by fruit and vine growing and by fishing. There are two harbours: at Loutra in the north, with a smallish hotel open in summer only, where are hot thermal springs coloured by iron deposits, and at Merihas on the west coast, also with a summer hotel. The little capital, Khora, with a number of small churches containing good ikons, lies inland towards the east coast; while the mediaeval capital, now abandoned, is beyond Loutra at the island's northern tip and boasts among its ruins a fine Byzantine church. A later former capital is Dhriopida, near the east coast, below which is the Kanála beach.

Siros

Siros, or Syra (pop. c. 20,000), capital of the prefecture of the Cyclades, is both their main commercial and industrial centre and also the busiest port, thanks to its extensive ship repair yards, though no longer a convenient island junction for changing shipping routes. Scenically it is agreeable if unsensational; historically it has a past obscure until the Middle Ages when a handful of Genoese and Venetian families gravitated there and settled, establishing it as a centre of the Roman Catholic faith — which it still is. The medieval quarter of the capital, Ano Siros, inland and to the north of the modern town, is enchanting, with its little Catholic churches sprinkled along steep whitewashed streets. Around it the hillsides are cultivated to grow early vegetables for the Athens market.

Ermoupolos

The port town, Ermoupolos, stretches back from the broad quayside that encircles the inner, commercial harbour. It has several good hotels. the waterfront is lined with grandiose 19th century buildings and busy *tavernas, kaffeneions* and shops. Behind it is the town centre, the large, elegant Plateia Miaoulis, to the north and west of which rise the capital's twin hills, the nearest one, Ano Siros, crowned by the Roman Catholic cathedral; the other (the Vrontado) by the Orthodox church of the Anastásis. From here there is a splendid view over the 19th century residential quarter, centred around the blue dome of Aghios Nikólaos, and over the entire harbour — the outer part of which, guarded by an islet, is full of ships waiting for repairs and refits, and ringed with small factories.

Outside the town there are attractive villages with bathing beaches, small hotels and *tavernas* at Kini on the west coast; at Dellagrazia (Poseidonia) and at Finikas, in the south-west; and at Vari and Mega Yialos in the south-east. All these can be reached by bus from Ermoupolis; the northern part of the island is mountainous and difficult of access, though there is an ancient site up at Khalandriani.

Mikonos

Mikonos and Dilos are invariably treated together, since the former is the traditional jumping-off place for the latter, which is only served (apart from cruise ships) by caiques from Mikonos when the weather permits — which is often not the case in the *meltemi* season. The two could hardly be more different in character, however. Mikonos, (pop. c. 5,500), in Classical times subject to Athens, later to Naxos, and later still to Venice, now belongs to international tourism and is the St Tropez of Greece. There are no beaches in the town itself; buses and boats serve nearly a dozen on the south and west coasts, some chiefly patronised by naturists or gays.

Mikonos Town

Virtually barren, nearly all its inhabitants live in the dazzling white harbour town of Mikonos which sits on a wide bay at the western tip of the island, backed by gentle hills. Its maze-like streets are crammed with boutiques of every description; there are dozens of hotels both in town and on various beaches *kaffeneions* and *tavernas* abound, spilling down to the wide waterfront.

More interesting than the boutiques are the dozens of little churches built by wealthy fishing families, of which the Paraportiáni, to the landward end of the quay, is the most-photographed. Aghia Kyriaki, just behind the harbour, has the best icons. The small archaeological museum (open daily, except Tuesdays, until mid-afternoon) exhibits Classical finds from Mikonos itself and from Rheneia, an island close to Dilos. A museum of Popular Art (open in the evenings) displays a traditional island home.

Dilos

Caiques for Dilos leave Mikonos at intervals throughout the morning, returning in the afternoons, taking about half an hour to reach the relatively calm channel between Dilos and Rheneia. But the service depends on wind conditions which in summer can halt it for days. It allows 2½-3 hours on Dilos; the ruins are open daily until mid-afternoon.

History
Venerated since the 10th century BC as the place where Apollo and his sister, Artemis, were born to Leto, Dilos had previously supported a Mycaenean community. It became the focal point of the so-called Delian League in the 7th century BC and was the site of important festivals and games. Down the centuries the wealthier city-states made offerings and established treasuries there, as at Delphi. In 490 BC the Persians forbore to attack it; after they were defeated Peisistratos of Athens ordered the sacred island to be purified: no one was permitted thereafter to give birth or to die there. Even today there are no inhabitants apart from caretakers and archaeologists.

By the late 4th century BC Dilos was becoming a rich trading port as well as a place of pilgrimage, and it continued in this role under the Romans, from the middle of the third century BC until 88 BC when it was sacked by the forces of Mithridates from Asia Minor. In the following year Rome achieved control again and rebuilt much of the town, but by the 3rd century AD Dilos was dwindling in importance and became an easy prey for the pirates and looters who roamed the Aegean thereafter, including treasure hunters in search of antiquities.

Today Dilos presents at first sight an appearance both desolate and awesome. Its low hills are covered with ruins, while the museum building and the one tourist pavilion (restaurant, bar and four bedrooms) are barely visible during the approach to the small mole that separates the ancient Sacred Harbour from the erstwhile commercial port. The ruins are so extensive and complex that they demand several visits, and deserve much more detailed description than falls within the scope of this guide.

The Lion Terrace
Briefly, however, the visitors' first inclination upon landing by the Sacred Harbour is to make straight for the famous Lion Terrace to the left (north). In doing so, they follow the paved Sacred Way, passing between the remains of Hellenistic *agoras* with their surrounding *stoas* and the bases of many statues. Visitors then cross the open space of the archaic Hieron of Apollo, once dominated by the huge marble statue of the god, of which part of the trunk remains and is identifiable, past a complex of Classical and Archaic temples on the right. Threading between more fallen masonry, they reach an avenue bounded on the east by the great bare expanse of the Stoa of the Italians and on the west by the Lion Terrace itself. Here five of the

great archaic beasts, carved in Naxian marble, sit erect and aloof, facing the sunken area that was once the Sacred Lake in the centre of which a palm tree commemorates the one beneath which Leto bore Apollo, the Sun God.

Touring the Ruins
Behind the lake and the shattered stonework are the remains of the Roman city wall, and behind this again stands the museum (same opening hours as the site) with some lovely Archaic and later statuary; reliefs; paintings; and pottery. The Tourist Pavilion is close by. To the south of these buildings the ground rises gently towards the low summit of Mount Kynthos (fine views). Below this, by the shore, is what is known as the Theatre Quarter, a concentration of mainly Hellenistic houses and workshops, several with splendid mosaics, grouped below a 3rd century BC theatre, from the top of which there are also good views. Just west of the theatre is a great cistern, and above it are more houses with mosaics, notably the House of the Masks and the House of the Dolphins. Further up the hillside again is the site of the 5th century BC Heraion, overlooking various Sanctuaries of Foreign Gods. The summit of the hill has yielded evidence of pre-historic habitation up to some 5,000 years old and is crowned by the remains of the Sanctuary of Zeus and Athena. Coming down again to the seashore, the onetime commercial harbour is edged with the outlines of store-rooms and wharf buildings.

Serifos

Serifos (pop. c. 1,200) is a small, and so far unexploited, oval upsurge of rockiness, broken wherever possible by carefully terraced vegetable gardens, productive thanks to a good supply of water. Legend has it that Danae and her son by Zeus, the infant Perseus, were rescued from the sea here, and after Perseus had grown to manhood and slain Medusa, he returned with its head and turned into stone the King Polydeuces, who was bent on seducing his mother. Its deep, tightly encircling harbour is Livadhi, on the east coast, served from Lavrion as well as Piraeus. Near it is a beach with a handful of small hotels. The capital, Khora, overlooked by a row of windmills, perches on a hill above it, about a mile inland. From Khora, tracks lead north-eastward to the sandy beach of Psili Ammos and, in the north of the island, to the 16th century Tachiarchou monastery with its collection of rare manuscripts. There are other excellent beaches at Megalo Livadhi on the west coast, Galini and Sikamia — all with summer *tavernas*.

Sifnos

Sifnos (pop. c. 2,200), some 13 kilometres (8 miles) south-east of Serifos, was renowned for its gold mines in antiquity, but Apollo laid a curse upon the Sifniots after they had deceitfully sent a gilded egg-shaped rock in place of a solid golden egg to his sanctuary at Delphi. Now this fertile, attractive island, dotted with ancient towers, fragmentary ruins and white-domed monasteries, among which are many attractive walks, is starting to work the tourist gold mine. Its capital, inland, is Apollonia, rising on a series of ridges and reached by bus from the harbour village, Kamares (inns, *tavernas*, apartments), served from both Piraeus and Lavrion. Attractive rustic pottery is made there. Below Apollonia, around the south coast, are the fine beaches of Platia Yialos (hotels, apartments, *tavernas*); Vathy and Faros (*tavernas*). The little Venetian-walled village of Kastro, built on the site of the ancient city above the east coast is dazzling-white; from its acropolis are views down to the sea and across to the island's second biggest village, Artemonas, typically Cycladic in appearance, with restaurants and *tavernas*.

Paros

Paros (pop. c. 8,000) rising evenly to one central mountain named Profitis Ilias, is one of the most popular tourist islands, well-served by ferries from Piraeus and Rafina. Although relatively treeless, there is a layer of fertile soil over the solid marble core that once made it famous. Parian marble was greatly prized in ancient times for its translucence, and the quarries with their underground tunnels can still be visited on the eastern slopes of Profitis Ilias.

According to legend, it was here that King Minos of Crete heard of the death of his son, Androgeus, by the hand of the Athenians — an act for which they were made to pay by sending youths and girls to be devoured by the Minotaur.

History
Paros has certainly been inhabited since the 7th century BC or earlier; later it sided with Persia during the wars and was punished by an Athenian force under Miltiades. This force, however, failed to take the island — a superstitious fear of the power emanating from the Sanctuary of Demeter is said to be the reason — and Miltiades died as the result of being wounded there. After the Persian defeat Paros did become an Athenian possession, and then a Roman one; in the Middle Ages it belonged to Naxos, and from the mid-16th century to the Ottomans, during which time it became a haunt of pirates. In the following century the "Parian Chronicle", now in the Ashmolean Museum, Oxford, listing the principal artistic achievements of ancient Greece in chronological order, was discovered here by a cleric in the service of the Duke of Arundel. Paros was liberated from Ottoman rule at the same time as the rest of the country.

Paros Town
The capital, Paros or Paroíkia, is a low whitewashed town, punctuated by blue church domes, that straggles along its waterfront on the west

coast of the island. It has several good hotels, *tavernas* and numerous *kaffeneions*, mostly along the quayside from where boats ply to and from the better beaches. Of its many churches, some with fine ikons, the most important is the Ekatontapiliani (Church of 100 Gates), said to have been founded upon a vow by St Helena; restored in the Byzantine style, it has later additions. Nearby is the museum (open daily, except Tuesdays, until mid-afternoon), exhibiting among other objects a fragment of the Parian Chronicle. At the other end of the town is a low hump of land with the remains of a Venetian *kastro* on it, partly built with masonry from the Sanctuary of Demeter, and beyond are the remains of an Asclepion. South of the town is the well-watered and rambling garden called Petaloudhes, covered in high summer by flocks of reddish-gold butterflies.

Other Resorts: Antiparos
Buses from Paros town run north-eastwards, past the Longovardhas monastery (closed to women) and through attractive fertile country-side to Naoussa. Grown from a fishing village into a fully-fledged popular resort (hotels, apartments, *tavernas*, etc.) it has several beaches and the remains of a castle built by the Dukes of Naxos. The marble quarries are along a road running further to the east and terminating, after passing through a couple of dazzling white hamlets, at Marpissa (hotels and *tavernas* below it) on the south-east coast. More beaches around the south coast are being developed, among them Driós, Aliki and Pounda. From there as well as from Paros town, boats cross the Antiparos, chiefly visited by for its stalactite caves.

Naxos
Naxos (pop. c. 14,000), well-served by ferries from Piraeus and Rafina, is the largest and most fertile of the Cyclades, and another marble island. In ancient times quarries were worked in the mountain spine that runs from north to south along its eastern flank, and beside them lie partly-worked pieces of statuary, though today it is better known for its pumice. The plains to the west and the foothills are fruitful with orange and olive groves, orchards and even cornfields, and Naxian wine and honey are both excellent. It was on Naxos that Theseus abandoned Ariadne, the daughter of King Minos of Crete.

Inhabited since earliest times, Naxos allied itself with Athens during the Persian wars and was the object of two Persian offensives; in the 4th century BC it became the battleground for Athens' defeat of the Lacedaemonians. Its greatest period, however, was in the Middle Ages when it was conquered by the Venetian pirate-king Marco Sanudi who established a dukedom there; this lasted for some 350 years until the Turks took the island in 1566.

Naxos Town
The capital, Naxos, lies piled on a low cone-like hill on the west side

of the island at the sea's edge. It has numerous hotels. Whitewashed and with many typically flat-roofed Cycladic houses to either side of its tortuous little streets, its upper part (the *kastro*) preserves a Venetian feel in the 13th century Cathedral and numerous fine old houses. At the end of a causeway leading off the end of the quay is an islet with a 15th century church and a massive archaic gateway that once led into a temple of Apollo. Just to the north of the town on the Aplomata hill are a whitewashed monastery and some Mycaenean cave-tombs. Finds from these, together with other archaeological treasures, are housed in the small museum in the former ducal palace (temporarily closed).

Inland, a web of roads, sometimes difficult to navigate thanks to erratic signposting, lead to high green valleys with small churches; villages distinguished by mediaeval tower-houses (Belonia, Halkí); Koronia and Apiranthos where emery is quarried. Above Apóllonas, to the north (beach inns, *tavernas*), lies a huge half-hewn Archaic *kouros* statue, still attached to the marble of the hill. Another road forks south-eastwards through the large white village of Tripodes, past Sangri with its relics both of Classical and Mediaeval times and south to Kastraki beach (*tavernas*).

Amorgós

Amorgós (pop. c. 1,800), the most easterly of the Cyclades, is served by ferries on the Dodecanese route that normally call at both at Katápola and Aighiáli, at opposite ends of the island. Long, narrow and hilly with particularly beautiful cliffs and beaches, it was the scene of Athens' final naval defeat by Macedon in 322 BC and the Romans later used it as a place of exile. Katápola on the west coast is really three villages strung into one and poised between olive groves and the deep sea gulf. Katápola has small inns and *tavernas*, but is scarcely developed. Above it are the remains of Minoa, one of the island's three main cities in antiquity. The present capital, Amorgós or Khora (inn), is across the narrow neck of the island and above the east coast; to the north of it, fantastically set against a cliff face, is the famous Khozoviótissa monastery which houses a miraculous ikon of the Panaghia (Virgin). North again is the Aigiali (inns, *tavernas*, beaches, all very simple). The ruins of ancient Aigiali are beyond it at the northern tip; the third city site of antiquity is Arkesine in the south, with a fine Hellenic tower.

Milos

Milos (pop. c. 3,800), to the south-west of Sifnos, lies around a huge north-facing bay, once the core of a long-sunken volcano. Its western half is dominated by the peak of the Profitis Ilias mountain, whilst the eastern part ripples away in low dry hills to the dependent islets of Kimolos, yielding quantities of the chalky Fuller's Earth used in making china, and Poliaigos. Milos has hot springs, sulphur mines and various mineral deposits,to which it owed its prosperity in ancient times.

Venus de Milo

The island, as well as being renowned for the Venus de Milo statue, appropriated by a French diplomat in 1820 and now in the Louvre, has contributed much to contemporary knowledge of Cycladic culture which flourished alongside the Minoan culture of Crete. It was prominent, too, in Mycaenean, Archaic and Classical times when it sided with Sparta against Athens and was sacked by the Athenians in retribution. During the Middle Ages it was occupied by the Franks, and then by the Turks.

Its port is Adhamas (inns, *tavernas*). Above the port and to the north is Milos, the charming capital (folk museum), surmounted by a Frankish *kastro* containing a 13th century Byzantine church on the site of the ancient capital. The "Venus" was found near a stretch of Hellenistic city wall just above the seaside hamlet of Klima; nearby are early Christian catacombs and a Roman theatre. Along the north coast road are the ruins of ancient Phylakopi, dating back to early Cycladic times; beyond it is the little fishing port of Vóudhia which has good beaches and *tavernas*. There is another good beach, Mavra Gremna, at the centre of the huge main bay; inland of it is the old capital, Chora (or Zefiria).

Kímolos

Excursions to Kímolos can be made from Vóudhia; it was a base for French priate ships in the 17th century and subsequently for more respectable French merchantmen. A French consular agent established there, Louis Brest, had a hand in negotiating the purchase of the Venus.

Folegándros and Sikinos

Lying between Milos and Ios, these islands are two of the driest of the Cyclades, stark and barren and thinly populated. Both are popular with yachtsmen seeking secluded bays, and with sub-aqua divers and snorkellers. Paleokastro, the tiny whitewashed main town of Folegándros, is situated inland of Karavostásis, the port, and below the site of the ancient city. It was sacked by the Turks and repopulated from the neighbouring islands during the 17th century. Its chief pride is the church of the Panaghia, with a miraculous ikon. Sikinos, its neighbour, is more fertile, with many vineyards. Its capital, Kastro, lies in the middle of the island around the foot of a rock crowned by the ruined Zoodokhos Pighi monastery. The port, such as it is, is Aloprónia on the east coast. Across from it, in the south-west, at Episkopi, once stood the so-called Temple of Apollo, its site now occupied by a late Byzantine church, while another ruined sanctuary lies at the northernmost tip of the island.

Ios

Ios (pop. c. 1,500) named after the Ionians who originally colonised it, lies midway between Naxos and Thera and is served by ferries from Piraeus. Partly depopulated earlier in this century by a tidal wave, it became popular with hippies who camped out on its fine beaches and squatted in deserted houses. Today its tourism is better organised and more remunerative, but still largely of the back-to-nature ethos. The island rises to two peaky hills in the centre; around them are terraced pastures and cornfields interspersed with tiny white chapels among olive groves. There are inns and *tavernas* at the port of Ormos Iou, or Skala, on the west coast, which has the good beach of Yialos alongside it. The capital, Ios, just uphill and inland of it and overlooked by windmills, has pretty churches and flanks the site of the ancient capital; many of its houses have been restored by foreigners, and much rebuilding has taken place. On the other side of the island the ruined 15th century Venetian Palaiokastro crowns a hilltop. Pretty beaches with hotels and *tavernas* are to be found below the Palaiokastro at Manganari. Milopotamos, near Yialos, has also been developed for tourism. The islanders' belief that Homer was buried here is almost certainly apocryphal.

Thera (Santorini)

Thera or Santorini (this latter being a corruption of the name of the island's patron saint, St Irene) is the southernmost island of the Cyclades group and one of the most important (pop. c. 7,500). It is well-served by ferries from Piraeus (car-ferries, too, occasionally) and has an airport that takes charter flights. It was once a volcano which in ancient times erupted catastrophically, possibly contributing to the destruction of the Minoan cities of Crete; its core then subsided beneath the sea. Thus the main part of the island now forms a semi-circle, partly completed by the islets of Therasia and Aspronisi, around a vast, deep lagoon where once rose the summit of the volcano. It is a weird sight, compounded by the strange-coloured striations that mark the high sheer sides of the crater-lagoon, and it has long been associated with the 'lost' continent of Atlantis. Two small larval islets lie within its broken circumference, but from the tops of the surrounding cliffs the land slopes away quite gently to the hamlets and dark sand beaches on the outer periphery of the island. The dry, volcanic soil bears particularly delicious tomatoes and grapes — Santorini red wine is renowned; pumice is the island's only other product.

Fíra

Passenger-ferries and cruise ships moor within the lagoon, landing passengers by tender at the foot of the cliff below the capital, Fíra. From thence a cable-car operates to the capital at the summit of the cliff: a welcome alternative to climbing hundreds of zigzagging steps, buffeted by the mules carrying the less-active or (worse still) riding one of the mules whose owners are a villainous and rapacious lot.

Fíra, seeming to teeter at the edge of the precipice, consists of a few parallel long, white streets along which are countless inns and hotels, a Roman Catholic and an Orthodox Cathedral. It also has numerous white-domed chapels, a newly built museum (open daily, except Tuesdays, until mid-afternoon) that houses many beautiful objects excavated on the island, including figures, pots, votives. There are scores of souvenir shops, a small carpet-weaving workshop, as well as *tavernas* and *kaffeneions* without end. On the outer edge of the town is a sizeable *plateia* from whence the few bus services and taxis operate to the peripheral parts of the island.

Oia
At the northern tip of the island the village of Oia (Ia), depopulated for many years, has come back to life thanks to tourism. It lies along a sharp ridge: a long, narrow cluster of dazzlingly white cubic houses, some half dug in to the cliff. Many of them restored for letting to tourists (the National Tourist Office has been instrumental in converting some). There are shops, *tavernas* and *kaffeneions* but it is considerably less frenetic than Fíra.

Ancient Thera
The two principal excursions are to ancient Thera, on a high saddle of land to the south-east, and to the Minoan site of Akrotiri to the south-west. As a city, ancient Thera dates back to the 10th century BC but most of its visible ruins are much later legacies, from the 2nd and 1st centuries BC, the Hellenistic era, when Egypt was in command of the southern Aegean. Long, narrow and complex, they stretch along a reinforced hilltop terrace bisected by one main street, off which open the *agoras*, courtyards and side streets, culminating in an Apollo temple, a Gymnasium and Roman baths. Below, on the shore, is the village of Périssa (hotels); another growing resort, Kamari, is a short way north.

Akrotiri
The Akrotiri site, just outside the village of the same name, which is dominated by a mediaeval fortress, is that of a large, wealthy township (some 30,000 inhabitants) of the Late Minoan period (about 1500 BC). It was buried beneath volcanic ash and thus remained extraordinarily well preserved: passageways have been tunnelled between rows of houses that in some places are two or more storeys high with clearly-delineated doors and window frames. In some respects the site's state of preservation can be compared to that of Pompeii or Herculaneum. But no skeletons were found: the citizens evidently had enough warning of the impending catastrophe to enable them to flee before their city died. The remarkably intact and exquisitely delicate frescoes found in some of the rooms were removed during excavation, restored, and placed on view in the National Archaeological Museum in Athens, along with some of the pottery and other objects found. They are eventually destined to return to a projected new museum

on Thera. Professor Spyridon Marinatos, excavator of Akrotiri, and propounder of the theory that the eruption of the Thera volcano caused the series of disasters that ended the Minoan civilisation, died on the site in 1974 and is buried there.

The monastery of Profitis Ilias, on the flank of its eponymous mountain, is no longer open to visitors but there are fine views from its vicinity and below it the fortified village of Pirgos and the church (11th century) of Episkopi Goniás are both of interest.

Therasia and Anafi

The Early Cycladic finds on Therasia have now been covered over; the island boasts a small cliff top hamlet but is otherwise of little interest. Nea Kaméni emits puffs of sulphurous smoke and Paleá Kaméni has warm-water springs bubbling offshore. All are visited on boat-excursions that also call at the tiny port below Oia. Anafi, a little island to the south-east, is seldom visited.

Crusader Castle, Rhodes

The Dodecanese
and
Eastern Aegean

The Dodecanese

The Dodecanese (Dodekánissa, meaning "twelve islands", was adopted at the end of the Turkish era to describe a political grouping which at the time did not include Rhodes or Kos, but now embraces fourteen islands) lie in the extreme south-east of the Aegean. Most of them flank the Asia Minor coast with Karpathos and Astypalaia slightly to their west. They are served from Piraeus by two main shipping routes, one via the Cyclades (Kiklades) and the other, more southerly, via Eastern Crete; ships also link them with Kavala and Thessaloníki in the north. Rhodes, Kos, Leros, Kastellórizo and Karpathos also have airports. All the islands enjoy a low rate of duty and taxes.

Rhodes
Rhodes, the largest (pop. c. 90,000) and best known, is also the furthest east but for Kastellórizo.

The Dodecanese and Eastern Aegean

A fish-shaped island, it is 85 kilometres (53 miles) long, with a mountainous central spine running roughly north-east to south-west and
becoming more rugged in the south. Rhodes is extremely mild climatically, even slightly humid, and also fertile, bearing citrus and other
fruits, nuts, and olives. It is covered in wild flowers and herbs in
spring and early summer — the plethora of rock-roses, especially,
having earned it its nickname of "Isle of Roses". There are also thick
pinewoods, particularly in the south-west; millions of butterflies and,
less publicised, snakes — only a very few of them harmful. There are
also numerous small fauna, including deer, and game in the hills.

History
In legend, it is supposed to have been created by the sun god, Helios,
on which to pursue his dalliance with the nymph Rhoda, and in prehistoric times its development was closely linked to those of Egypt, Asia
Minor, Crete and Mycaenae. By the dawn of the Classical Age in the
6th century BC its three city-states, Lindos, Kameiros and Ialysos,
were already rich and powerful, siding successively with Persia, Sparta
and Egypt against Athens and, later, Rome. The city of Rhodes itself
was founded in 408 BC, jointly by the three older cities; being ambitiously conceived and planned, it flourished immediately. It was an
important artistic centre in Classical and Hellenistic times, as well as
a leading naval and marine trading power. Rhodes became part of the
Byzantine Empire in the 4th century AD and, after this empire fell,
came into Venetian and then Genoese hands. The Knights of St John,
originally an order of hospitallers who gradually became militarised,
conquered the island in 1309 and ruled it for over 200 years until
forced to flee to Malta by the Turks. The Ottoman Empire then took
control until ousted by the Italians during the war of 1911-12, and
Rhodes belonged to Italy, along with the other Dodecanese, until after
World War II.

Rhodes New Town
The capital, Rhodes (Rodos), at the northern tip of the island, is divided
into two parts: the old town, encircled by the massive mediaeval
walls of the former fortress, and the new one built by the Italians,
which stretches away westward of it, past the harbour of Mandraki
and along the seashore. The extrance to Mandraki, where once stood
the Colossos of Rhodes, is now guarded by two bronze deer on pillars;
on the east mole stand three windmills and a round tower. Opposite
Mandraki is a picturesque Turkish partly-covered food market, the
New Market, and to the west of it are the Cathedral, the portentous
public buildings, a mosque whose cemetery contains graves of many
Muslim notables, and the Aquarium. For the rest, the new town consists mainly of hotels, scores of them in all categories; a casino;
shops, restaurants and cafes, many of these latter facing the shrub-
planted pleasantly Italianate espalanade that extends westward from
Mandraki to the Aquarium.

Rhodes Old Town
The main approach to the Gothic Old City, restored by Mussolini's
Italians, is through a garden behind the Mandraki mole. Off this opens
an Italian-built gateway giving on to the former Castle of the Knights.

To the right of the courtyard, within, are the remains of a Hellenistic
temple of Aphrodite; in the centre is a Byzantine fountain; heaped
here and there are cannon balls dating back to the 16th century Turkish
siege. Around are restored mediaeval buildings, one housing a
Museum of Decorative Arts (open three mornings weekly). Beyond,
through an archway, is the former Hospital of the Knights, now an
Archaeological Museum (open daily, except Tuesdays, until mid-afternoon). This impressive building, broken by more courtyards, houses
memorials of the Knights; sculpture, including the Roman Aphrodite
of Rhodes, and the earlier Venus Pudica; funerary reliefs; mosaics;
Mycaenean jewellery, and pottery. The cobbled Street of the Knights
(Ippoton) leads uphill from the museum, flanked by restored mediaeval
mansions that are largely obscured, like others in the adjacent streets,
by tight-packed souvenir shops. At the top of the hill is the Palace of
the Grand Masters (open day-long except Tuesdays), entirely rebuilt
by Mussolini with a view to occupying it himself, and containing
ancient mosaic pavements from Kos. From here also starts the tour
of the ramparts (Mondays and Saturdays at 1430).

Turkish Quarter
Uphill of the Palace, the Amboise Gate, preceded by a busy little
square, leads across the grassy moat to the upper part of the New
Town. By turning left in the square and not going through the gate,
one leaves the knightly precincts of the old City and, following
Sokratous Street, passes the attractive Suleiman Mosque and the old
Turkish bazaar quarter with picturesque narrow streets, criss-crossed
by the buttresses of inter-supporting houses and dotted with derelict
mosques and mediaeval buildings. Tourist shops, restaurants and
cafés become thicker on the ground at the bottom of the hill, where
two typical squares are adorned with attractive fountains. Gates from
this lower part of town lead to the quayside of the commercial port.

Outside the city to the east is the neo-Moorish spa resort of Kallithea
and the booming beachside resort of Faliraki.

Western Rhodes
The great sweep of Triandha Bay, to the west, is lined with enormous
tourist hotels, many of them standing behind the main coast road.
Above them rises the flat-topped hill of Fileremos where are the ruins
of ancient Ialysos, partly overlaid by a Byzantine chapel and later
mediaeval buildings.

Beyond this, the west coast road runs through a string of little villages,
past the turning to Petaloúdhes, a valley where butterflies congregate

en masse in high summer, past the airport, and on to the ruins of Kámeiros, one of the three ancient Rhodian cities. Its remains (open daily until mid-afternoon), sprawl up a low hill overlooking the sea, and culminate in a 3rd century BC Doric colonnade from which there are fine views. Less visited than Lindos, it nevertheless makes a pleasant excursion and there are *tavernas* with changing-facilities on the neighbouring beaches.

Beyond Kámeiros, the coast road runs down to Kritinia, below which is a dramatically-situated Knights' castle. A side road just before Kámeiros winds inland through pine forests around the base of the Profítis Ilias mountain (hunting); it can be followed on into the foothills of Mt Ataviros, to the village of Embona which keeps much of its traditional atmosphere. After Embona (and south of Kritinia on the coast, which is connected with it), the mostly well-surfaced southbound road that now loops round to ring the island, reveals the contrast between the ultra-commercial north and the lovely, undeveloped south. En route, a short detour at Monólithos leads to another dramatic Knights' castle, or *frourio,* with a little chapel in its ruined *enceinte.*

Eastern Rhodes
After Katavia, southernmost village on Rhodes, the road winds back north through Genádio and Lárdos, both being developed for tourists, towards Lindos where it meets the east coast highway. In Lindos itself, cars are not allowed and must be parked on the road leading down to the beach and its scores of fast-food and more pretentious restaurants, bars, cafes and *tavernas.* At the edge of the village is a shady square with *kaffeneions,* from which the route to the Acropolis is blazed with tourist shops. You can hire donkeys for the ascent. The Acropolis itself (open every day, all day long) is finally reached via a flight of steps and through a mediaeval gateway built by the Knights. On it are the 3rd, 4th and early 5th century BC remains of the Sanctuary of Athena Lindia, and a Byzantine chapel, breathtakingly perched above the sea with marvellous views. Descending again, the narrow, cobbled alleyways of the village are lined with old houses that are rented out to tourists; restaurants and shops abound.

Symi; Tilos; Kastellórizo; Nisyros
Between Rhodes and Kos lie three small islands, dry and rocky, each with a ruined mediaeval fortress guarding it: Symi, Tilos and Nisyros. Symi, famous for its sponge fishers, and in antiquity for its ship-builders (it sent three ships to the Trojan War), has a beautiful many-tiered neo-Classical town that has adapted itself gracefully to tourism. There are splendid views from the top, which has a more Cycladic air. The town has a few small hotels and many houses for rent; an 18th century monastery on the southwest coast makes an interesting excursion by boat. Tilos, Kastellórizo, to the southeast of Rhodes, and Nisyros, an extinct volcano, have so far escaped mass tourism; none

at the time of writing even has an hotel, though there are rooms for rent on all three.

Kos

Kos, the second largest of the Dodecanese (pop. c. 21,000) with its tip only 2 kilometres (1¼ miles) from the Turkish coast at Bodrum, is a smaller-scale version of Rhodes: long and narrow, hilly to the south, well watered and fertile. Although inhabited from earliest times, its fame in antiquity centred entirely around its Sanctuary of Asclepios, and the medical school founded in honour of Hippocrates, who was born there in the 5th century BC. After its conquest by Alexander the Great in 336 BC, Kos became a rich trading centre that passed to Egypt on Alexander's death and eventually became part of Roman Asia Minor. Thereafter its history in Byzantine, mediaeval, and more recent times, parallels that of Rhodes.

Kos Town

The principal town, Kos, is a modern but attractive and cosmopolitan Italianate port, well planted with trees and flowers, at the north-eastern end of the island. A vast Castle of the Knights (open daily, except Tuesdays, until mid-afternoon), protects the eastern flank of its harbour; a Roman *agora,* an Odeum, baths and Roman houses (one of them reconstructed), some with good mosaics, lie in little oases among the streets: you could come across a different one each day for a week or more. At the Castle end of the waterfront is Plateia Platanou with the enormous "plane tree of Hippocrates" — in fact not nearly old enough to have been contemporary — at its centre. Beside it is a pretty fountain and an elegant former mosque. The museum (open daily, except Tuesdays, until mid-afternoon) is at the heart of the town, behind the waterfront. There are many hotels, big and small, some in town and others on the beaches to either side of it, most within walking distance of the town centre; *tavernas* and *kaffeneions* also abound, particularly along the quayside and there is the usual complement of tourist shops.

The Rest of Kos

The principal sight on the island, the Asclepeion, lies some 2 kilometres (1¼ miles) to the south-east of the town, terraced up a gentle hillside at the end of a shady avenue of cypresses. There are remains, mostly Hellenistic and much-restored by the Italians, of baths and temples: white columns among the surrounding greenery, with splendid views of the Turkish mainland from the higher points. Other excursions on the islands are to Asfendioú and its neighbouring old villages up in the hills among woods and streams; Old Pili with its ruined Byzantine castle and village; the mediaeval castle of Antimakhia near the airport. At the island's south-western tip, below the village of Kefalos, is the small beach resort of Kamari (with a large Club Med beyond it) and the fine undeveloped Aghios Stephanos beach. Below

Aghios Fokas, on the south-east tip of the island, is a spa. Kardamena, near the airport in the south, has a good beach, hotels, inns and *tavernas;* it is the island's principal beach resort although development is also taking place along the north coast.

Kalymnos

Kalymnos (pop. C. 14,200), shaped like an upturned comma, is the most famous sponge-fishing island. Its capital, Pothia, clambers upwards from a deep bay on the south coast; its houses have been painted predominantly in blue and white — the Greek national colours — since the days of Italian rule, as a gesture of defiance. There are several inns and *tavernas.* Behind the town a road threads through a lovely valley, passing first beneath a hill topped with windmills and a ruined Castle of the Knights (core of the former capital), and then by some scattered antiquities, and dipping finally down to the sheltered double-headed bay of Myrtiés with its hamlets, small summer hotels and bungalows, *tavernas,* good swimming.

Telendos

Offshore is the tiny islet of Telendos, with another tiny hamlet, Greek and Roman remains, and a ruined mediaeval castle and monastery; along its coast can be seen the outlines of old houses that have sunk beneath the sea. The east coast of Kalymnos, around Vathy, is also pretty.

Leros

Leros, another sponge-fishing island (pop. c. 9,000), has a sharply-indented coastline rising to an interior of beautifully contoured low hills. Known in antiquity, and linked with the other Dodecanese in mediaeval times, it became an important naval base during Italian domination and was briefly occupied by the British in World War II. Its principal port is Laki (ferries from Piraeus), where there are inns and *tavernas,* on a huge enclosed bay in the south-west; on the east coast is the capital, Aghia Marina, overlooked by a steeply-perched Castle of the Knights. There are good beaches nearby, notably Alinda (inns, *tavernas,*). Other beachside hamlets beginning to attract tourists after a period when the island was out of bounds to all but political prisoners of the military junta, are Panteli and Gournas, but Leros is by no means chasing mass-tourism.

Patmos

Patmos (pop. c. 2,700), most northerly of the Dodecanese, is shaped almost like an ink blot. No longer as arid as in former ages, Patmos is nonetheless largely barren, with only a few pines, gums, olives and fruit trees to soften its sharp hills. That it was scantily settled in antiquity is known, but its chapter in history really opens in the first century AD when it was used as a place of exile and received the banished St John the Divine (whom some identify with the Apostle John). Here St John wrote the Book of Revelations and here, ten centuries of neglect and piracy later, the Blessed Christodoulous was, in 1088, permitted by the Byzantine Emperor to found a monastery in the saint's honour.

Monastery

On a deep curvy gulf almost cutting the island in two from the east stands Skala, the commercial centre and chief port (ferries from Piraeus); the huge, polygonal fortified monastery with its buttressed grey stone walls crowns the hill above, ringed about by the whitewashed houses of Khora. A metalled road (buses and taxis) and a cobbled mule- and foot-path lead up from Skala to the final stepped ascent to the monastery (feast day May 21st). Its charming entrance courtyard flanks the church, and is one of the many enlargements and additions made since its foundation. The Founder's Chapel contains a fine silver reliquary, and from it an ancient portal opens into the main part of the church, whose mosaic floor is original. Off it is a small chapel with austere 12th century frescoes; there are also frescoes (13th century) in the refectory.

The treasury contains many rich and important items including crosses, chalices and embroidered robes; above it is the library with magnificent early manuscripts and ikons. Above this again, the roof terraces have marvellous views across the flat grey roofs of Khora, of the island itself and the surrounding Aegean.

Khora and Skala

Khora is a mass of steep narrow streets and white houses, some a century or more old, and dozens of little churches. It is pleasant to walk down from there in the evening, stopping at the Monastery of the Apocalypse which has grown up around the cave in which St John, according to tradition, had his Revelation. It has been converted into a simple chapel, with a chapel of St Anne alongside it.

Skala, with a pretty Italianate arcaded *plateia* fronting the quay and proliferating tourist shops, small hotels, *tavernas* and *kaffeneions*, is cheerful and appealing. From it little boats ply to the bathing beaches: Lambis in the north and Kambos (*tavernas* on both); Grikou (inns and *tavernas*) to the south-west. A boat trip round the entire island is also possible in a day.

Astypalaía

Astypalaía and Kárpathos are the remaining two Dodecanese of any size; they lie to the west of the main group, the former linking it to the Cyclades. Astypalaía is shaped like an H, with huge bays to north-west and south-east of its isthmus cross-bar; the southerly one, Maltezana, being the best sheltered. The island has a long history: it was the home of the giant, Kleomedes, who killed his wrestling opponent at Olympia and was banished, and it was used as a naval base by the Romans. In the Middle Ages it was the domain of the Quirini family, who called it Stampaglia and their *palazzo* in Venice still bears this name; it fell to the Turks in 1522 after over 300 years of Quirini rule. The Quirini *kastro*, enclosing a maze of narrow streets lined with wood-balconied houses, juts up above the capital of Khora, which in turn is just above and almost part of the little port of Periyalo, on Maltezana Bay, which has several small inns, *tavernas* and *kaffeneions*.

There is a small beach in town and another on the other side of the *kastro* promontory at the edge of a fertile valley; others, mostly pebbly, string out north along the bay as far as Analipsi.

Karpathos

More interest is packed into a small area on Karpathos than on most other minor Greek islands. Until recently it was hard to get to although it lies like a stepping-stone between Rhodes and Crete. Now there are not only local flights to supplement the ferries from Rhodes but charters from Britain as well. It is a comparatively wealthy island; since property has always been handed down through the female line, the surplus men have emigrated to work in the United States and Australia and returned to live off generous pensions. It may not, however, be rich enough to afford to turn its back on mass tourism; much new building is taking place in and around Karpathos town, also called Pighadia, and at the port of Diafáni in the north, though to date it is small-scale.

Pighadia (Karpathos Town)
Pighadia, at the south-eastern end of this long, narrow and mountainous island, is the lively capital, with plenty of small hotels, *tavernas* and other facilities. Behind the promontory against which it is built is a trio of excellent beaches at Amopi (pensions, *tavernas*), and in the hills above is Menetes, a handsome village the church of which can be seen for miles; it contains a fine carved iconostasis and ancient columns.

Western Karpathos
Down on the opposite (south-west) coast is Arkasa, with more beaches to either side of a huge Mycaenean fortress and a tiny chapel on the site of a 5th century basilica, with 5th century fragments built into it and the remnants of mosaics.

Further up the west coast is the tiny port of Finikí; then the hamlet of Lefkos just above a sensational triple-headed bay of pale sand beaches (*tavernas*). In the foothills above are the engaging villages of Mesohori and Othos, the latter with a charming folk-museum in an old

Karpathian mansion.

Eastern Karpathos
More beautiful beaches flank the east coast, reachable by boat but occasionally visible from the roughish road that winds northwards along the island's spine. It goes through the village of Aperi, said to be the richest on the island and full of imposing houses built by returned *emigrés*, and climbs through mountains thickly forested with pines (in places rendered sadly ghostlke by fires). The village of Olimbos, plastered against the mountains with a row of windmills above it, is at the end of the road and almost another world; here all but the young girls wear the traditional female dress of black head-scarf, black embroidered cloak over white embroidered cotton shift, and tall, soft leather boots. Corn is ground by one of the windmills, bread baked in outdoor ovens; the church, with faded 18th century frescoes and a heavily-carved iconostasis, smells of incense. Houses, reminiscent of the Othos folk-museum, have raised platforms at the rear of the ground floor where the family sleeps; by day, the bedding is covered with home-embroidered cloths. Twentieth-century comforts include TV sets and proper plumbing, and many houses have upper storeys with rooms to let.

Down on the coast, reached by a well-surfaced road, the small port of Diafáni has many pensions and *tavernas* and a long shingly beach; day-excursion boats from Pighadia deposit their passengers at its mole.

Eastern Aegean Islands
The Eastern Aegean islands (or Eastern Sporades) continue the line of the Dodecanese, paralleling the Turkish coastline. Southernmost of them are Samos and Ikaria, completing the island stepping-stones between the Greek mainland and Asia Minor.

Samos
Samos (pop. c. 41,000) which has air and sea services to Athens and Piraeus, is nearest to Turkey of all the Greek islands (seasonal boat connections with Kusadasi), and lies at right angles to it, bisected by a spine of mountains. Pines grow on the upper slopes and below them olives, fruit and vines are cultivated: Samian wine, the red variety in particular, the recipe of which is supposed to have originated with Bacchus, is famous and perhaps partly responsible for the island's growing tourism.

History
In antiquity Samos was also renowned for its wealth, its brilliance and its Hera cult which was probably introduced by its very earliest

157

settlers. By the 7th century BC the island was founding colonies all along the Asia Minor coast, and reached its zenith under the tyrant Polykrates in the 6th century BC. The huge Heraion (temple of Hera) was built in his reign; also the harbour mole and the Efpalínion underground aqueduct — all greatly admired throughout the ancient world.

Samos was conquered during the Persian wars, but ended on the side of Athens: the last naval battle of the conflict was fought in the Straits of Mikali which separate the island from Asia Minor. Thereafter it was dominated by Athens, Sparta, Macedon and finally by the Romans — Cicero was pro-Consul there, and Antony and Cleopatra sojourned there. Byzantines, Arabs, Venetians, Turks and Russians succeeded the Romans, and Samos was not reunited with Greece until 1912.

Its most famous sons were the 6th century BC mathematician Pythagoras, a later sculptor of the same name, Epicurus the philosopher and Aristarchos, the 3rd century BC astronomer who first discovered that the earth moved round the sun.

Samos Town
The capital consists of the twin towns of Samos, with hotels and *tavernas*, on a deep bay in the north, and Vathy, uphill of it. The main street meanders behind the waterfront; there is a palm-shaded *plateia*, a pretty public garden, and a museum (open daily, except Tuesdays, until mid-afternoon) containing Archaic stone torsos, small terracotta and bronze figures, and pottery. Buses serve neighbouring beaches and other island villages.

Pithagório
The ancient capital was on the south coast: the charming port of Pithagório (after Pythagoras), dominated by a 19th century basilica, lies over part of it. It is well-developed as a resort, with many small hotels and *tavernas*. The harbour mole is built on top of Polykrates' foundations and the entrance to the extraordinary 6th century BC tunnel-aqueduct, boring over 1,000 metres through a hill, is just behind Pithagório. Beyond the village and the little airport, near a long shingly beach, is a solitary incomplete column rising out of an awesome mass of ancient masonry that was once the Heraion: the goddess Hera is said to have been born in the nearby river. Buildings from all ages lie shattered around it and excavations still continue: it has one of the longest documented histories of any ancient religious site.

The Rest of Samos
The main road round the island climbs up behind it through Khora, the one-time Turkish capital, and twists westward through the hills past Marathókampos (beach, hotels, etc., below it) to Karlovassi, a large village with hotels, *tavernas* and a sizeable port. The road then runs back eastwards to Vathy along a north coast corniche that touches

several attractive villages and fine pebble beaches.

Samos has a number of monasteries: Vrondiani, the oldest, dates back to the 16th century and lies inland of the north coast; Zoodokhos Pighi (18th century) and the slightly older Aghia Zoni are near Vathy at the eastern end.

Ikária

Ikária, which has infrequent boats from Piraeus, is the largest of Samos's dependencies, lying midway between it and the eastern-most Cyclades. Fertile, well timbered and windy, it is named for Icarus, son of Daedalus the labyrinth maker. Escaping Crete with his father, Ikária marks the spot where he plummeted into the sea when the sun melted the wax that held his home-made wings together. The island capital is Aghia Kirikos in the south-east, but the neighbouring spa of Therma to the north of it and Loutra to the south (radioactive hot springs) are the main resorts, now embarking on a mini-boom; Evdilos on the north coast is also becoming popular. Ikária is also known for its apricots, its honey, and a scatter of fragmentary ruins.

Khios (Chios)

Khios (pop. c. 51,000) has air and sea connections with Athens and Piraeus, and seasonal boat connections with Çesme in Turkey. Crescent-shaped, with its inward-curving shore facing the Aegean, it lies north of Samos and close to the Asia Minor coast. The lower slopes of the volcanic chain that cuts it in two are thickly cultivated with olives, fruit, vines and, above all, lentisk trees. These are "milked" for their mastic, which is used to make both chewing gum and the sweet *mastica* liqueur: mastic — and successful shipowners — are today the best-known products both of Khios and its tiny dependency, Psara.

History

In antiquity, however, Khios was as brilliant culturally as Samos and claims Homer, among others, as a son. It shares a similar history with Samos, though it freed itself from Persia before its sister island, and was less subservient to Athens afterwards. St Paul paid a visit but, after the fall of Byzantium, it succumbed to various marauding powers until partially revived by the Genoese in the 14th century. In 1566 the Turks took possession for over 250 years and, when the Khiots rose against them in the War of Independence, massacred the population. It returned to the Greek fold in 1912.

Khios Town: Nea Moni

Khios, the capital, sits on the edge of a plain facing the Turkish coast on the site of the ancient city. It is a large flattish town; its one hill, crowned by a crumbling Genoese castle, the *frourio*, has old Turkish houses within its walls. The rest of the town, centred round Plateia Vounaki, also bears architectural witness to Turkish occupation, with jutting wooden balconies and occasional mosques. One of these now houses the little museum (open daily, except Tuesdays, until mid-afternoon) with pots and other finds from local sites. There are several hotels in the town, which is busy and urban; others along the shore to the north of it.

Outside the town above the village of Kariyés, is the 11th century convent church of Nea Moní the brilliant mosaics of which, together with those of Daphni and Osios Loukas, are among the finest examples of Byzantine art in the country.

Southern Khios
In the southern part of the island, an equally rewarding excursion is through the hills to the fortified mediaeval village of Pirgí at the centre of the mastic-growing country. Its curiously decorated house façades, covered in *sgraffito*, are grouped around the small main square and along some of the narrow cobbled side streets. The little Aghioi Apostoli church, near the main square, also has good frescoes. Mesta, nearby, is an entirely fortified village, entered by tunnels beneath the encircling houses (some of which have been restored by the National Tourist Office for letting to tourists).

Beyond Pirgí, on the south coast, are the ruins of an Archaic temple of Apollo at Kato Fano; further east are the Early Bronze Age remains of Emborió, partly under water: the first to be excavated (in 1954) using sub-aqua equipment. There are inns and *tavernas*; the swimming is good.

Northern Khios
To the north of Khios town the main coast road passes through Vrontadós, where a vast hewn-stone cube is said to have served Homer as a seat when discoursing to his pupils. The road goes on through the fishing village of Langadha to the pretty two-tiered hill town of Khardhámila in the north with good beaches, an inn, and *tavernas* below it. A branch off this road at Vrontadós leads past the 9th century monastery of Aghios Isidoros to Vólissos, claiming to be Homer's birthplace (beach, inns, boats to Psara), and to the Moní Aghias Markéllas beyond.

Lesbos (Mytilini)
Lesbos, third largest of the Aegean islands (pop. c. 88,500), has air services to Athens and Thessaloníki, ferry services to Thessaloníki, Kavala, Kymi and Piraeus. Its airport also takes charter flights. It is cleft by two balloon-shaped gulfs to the south, between which the land rises to its highest. It is extremely beautiful and fertile in the south and east, particularly with olives, which produce excellent

quality oil.

History
Its history is closely linked with that of Asia Minor: it took Troy's part in the Trojan War and, in later times, allied itself against Athens — first with Persia and then, briefly, with Sparta. Its principal cities, Mytilini and Mithimna (Mólivos), were perpetual rivals, weakening the island's power, and its later history is one of successive domination by its former allies, Sparta and Persia; then by Macedon, Egypt, Anatolia, Rome, Byzantium, Venice, Genoa and the Ottoman Empire. It has always had strong traditions of literature and female independence, both personified by the 7th century BC poet Sappho; more recently it has gained further fame through the primitive modern painter Theophilos and the poet Odysseas Elytis, winner of the 1979 Nobel Prize for Literature.

Mytilini
The capital, Mytilini, is a pleasant if undistinguished modern port town, with several hotels, good restaurants and *kaffeneions*, rising gently from the east coast to a Genoese *kastro*. The ancient city lies buried beneath it, but there is a Roman theatre at its edge, and the remains of the old city walls. There is a good small museum in town (open daily, except Tuesdays, until mid-afternoon), beaches just south of it, and much to explore beyond.

Southern Lesbos
The main road west out of Mytilini skirts the narrow Gulf of Yera and forks right into the hills. There are partly-submerged remains of an ancient port just past Thermai Yera. Up a side turning is the shady village of Aghiássos where they make pottery and some women still wear traditional dress; the 14th century Koimiséous tou Theotókou monastery has fine ikons. The main road winds on below, in the lee of a mediaeval fortress, to Poliknitos, sitting amid salt flats on the Kalloni Gulf, and beyond it to the vast beach of Vatera on the south coast.

Northern Lesbos
The same road out of Mytilini, passing the Aghiássos fork, skirts the Kalloni Gulf and arrives at the fishing port of Kalloni, a major crossroads. From here, a long circuit to the west takes in Antissa, Sigri and the extraordinary offshore petrified forest between it and Eressós, birthplace of Sappho, with some Archaic, Roman and Byzantine ruins. The village of Skala Eressos, beyond it, is developing into a modest resort.

The northerly route out of Kalloni squeezes through lovely hills and crosses a fertile plain on the shores of which lie Petra with a charming church (Panaghia Glykofiloássa) perched on a rock, and a long coarse sand beach. The road ends at the island's northern tip, in Míthymna (or Mólivos) where are hotels, inns, rooms in private houses and *tavernas*. This enchanting village, carefully conserved and popular with painters, spills down from a Genoese castle to a pretty port and a long, pebble beach; it is the principal tourist resort on Lesbos.

Eastern Coast

A rough road from here runs inland of the northernmost hills and passes through Mandamadhos, which has an inn; the Tahiárkhou church possesses a remarkable ikon that is the focus of a curiously pagan springtime festival. On the way there is a turn-off for Sikamineá, a minute and picturesque fishing port with a couple of pensions and *tavernas*. Thereafter, the road rejoins the eastern shore, goes through Loutra Thermis, a spa village on the site of an ancient city (hotels) and bypasses the village of Moria, with its Roman aqueduct, before returning to Mytilini.

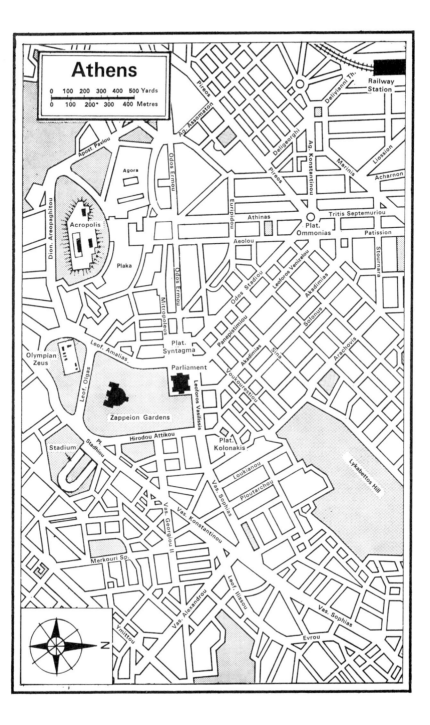

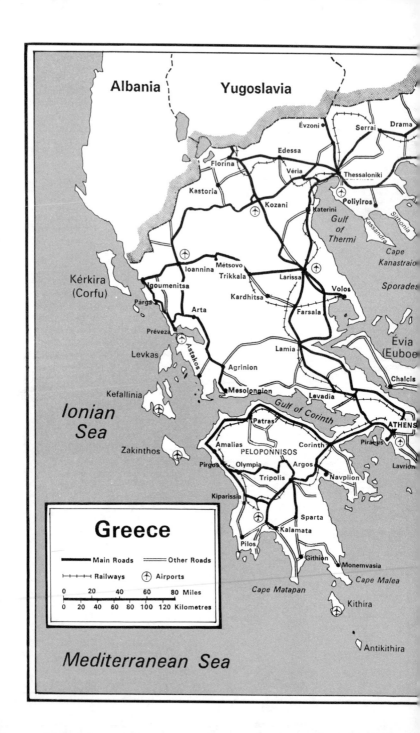

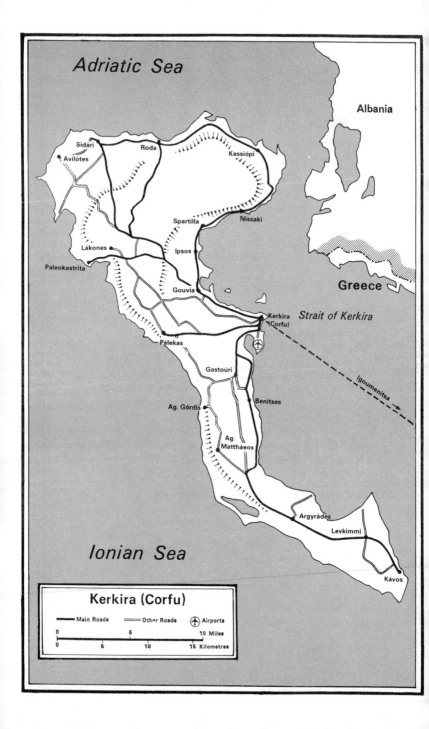

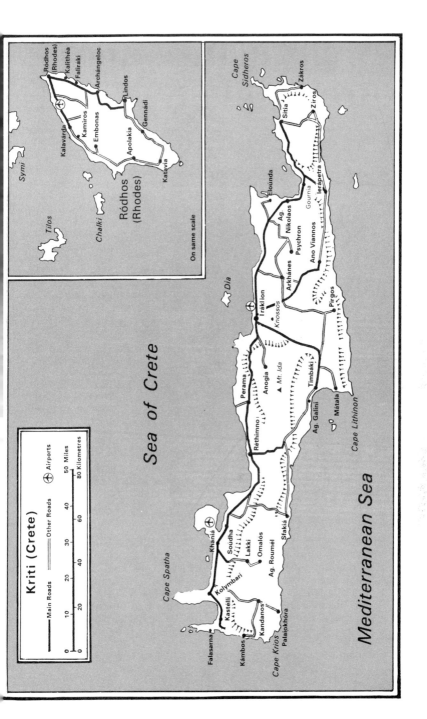

Kriti (Crete)

Main Roads
Other Roads
⊕ Airports

| 0 | 10 | 20 | 30 | 40 | 50 Miles |
| 0 | 20 | 40 | 60 | 80 Kilometres |

Sea of Crete

Mediterranean Sea

Cape Spatha

Khaniá
Soudha
Kolymbari
Kastélli
Kándanos
Kámbos
Falasarna
Cape Krios
Palaiokhóra
Lakki
Omalós
Ag. Roumél
Sfakia

Perama
Rethimno
Anogia
▲ Mt. Ida
Timbáki
Ag. Galini
Mátala
Cape Lithinon

Iráklion
Knossos
Arkhánes
Ano Viannos
Psychron
Pirgos

Elounda
Ag. Nikolaos
Ierápetra
Gournia

Cape Sidheros
Sitia
Zíros
Zákros

Dia

Symi
Tilos
Chalki

Ródhos (Rhodes)

Rodhos (Rhodes)
Kalithéa
Faliráki
Archángeloc
Lindos
Kamiros
Embonas
Kalavárda
Apolakia
Gennadi
Katávia

On same scale

Architecture and Archaeology

Classical Greek Architecture

The Classical Greek Temple

The Greek temple, originally built around the site of an altar, was designed to hold an image of the God or Goddess which it honoured.

The architecture was structurally simple, with proportions set by the 'module', which was the average radius of a column. The length of a temple was twice its width. However the design was more subtle than it appears. The columns leaned inwards very slightly and the centres of entablatures were higher than the extremities, so that they should appear precisely straight to the human eye. The stonework was painted in bright colours, such as reds and blues, and the roofs were made of wood or thatch.

There were three main orders of architecture. The Doric, illustrated here and in the photograph of the Temple of Apollo at Bassae on page 35, had the simplest elements with the columns set straight on to the temple floor, or stylobate. Each column had 20 flutes. The style developed among the Dorians of the mainland.

ELEMENTS OF A
TEMPLE PORTICO

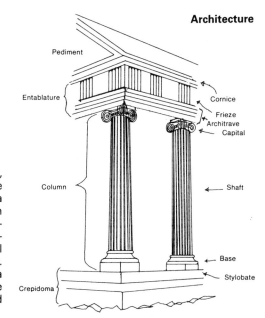

Pediment

Entablature

Cornice
Frieze
Architrave
Capital

Column

Shaft

The Ionic order, developed by the Ionians of Asia Minor after the 5th Century BC, is notably more sophisticated and graceful than its predecessor. The capitals had a 'double-scroll' while the pediment had decorated cornices.

Base

Stylobate

Crepidoma

About the same time the Corinthian was derived from the Ionic, its characteristic feature being acanthus leaves carved round the capitals of the columns.

As the architecture developed, elements which were originally of wood, like the pediment supporting the tiled roof, came to be executed in stone, but kept their old design.

Sculpture played an important part in architecture from a very

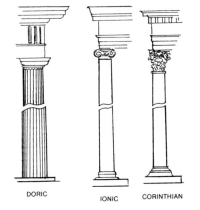

DORIC

IONIC   CORINTHIAN

Architecture

Caryatids

THÓLOS

GREEK THEATRE GROUND PLAN

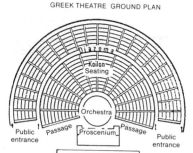

Scena (often disappeared)

TEMPLE GROUND PLAN

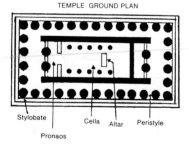

Stylobate   Cella   Altar   Peristyle
Pronaos

early time, reaching an apogee in the 5th Century BC when Pheidias carved the relief marble figures for the Parthenon (now in the British Museum and the Louvre). The famous caryatids of the Erectheion in Athens (see illustration and page 33) were subsidiary columns in the shape of draped female figures. (These have been replaced by copies and the originals will be displayed in a new Acropolis Museum planned for the 1990s).

The Tholos
This was a circular temple, usually built for commemorative reasons.

Theatres
Open air theatres were first built to house religious spectacles. Ritual dances to the God Dionysos were held in the circular orchestra. Gradually these evolved into performances of comedy and tragedy. Originally constructed of wood, after the 4th Century BC theatres were made of stone. Tiers of seats looked across the orchestra to the proscenium a portico framing the scena or stage. These have now disappeared from most remaining theatres, the best examples of which are at Argos, Athens, Delphi, Dodona and Epidauros.

Krater

Vases

The decoration of clay vases with painted scenes of human action and mythology was an important art form in ancient Greece and provides a unique insight into its life and civilisation. Of many vase styles two of the most popular were the amphora and the krater, both basically used for storing wine.

Amphora

Byzantine Churches

The Greek cross provided the basic shape for the Byzantine church. The walls forming the cross supported a dome representing the heavens and stood within the square of the whole building. The 'cross-in-square' sometimes had a porch and an outer porch added to it. The design reached its height in the 10th and 11th Centuries AD at the monasteries of Daphni and Osias Loukas (see photographs pages 34 and 36).

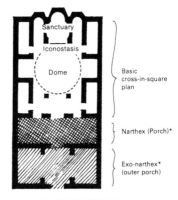

BYZANTINE CHURCH GROUND PLAN

*Not always present

Principal Archaeological Periods

Neolithic	before 3000 BC
Pre-Hellenic or Bronze Age	3000 - 1100 BC (includes Minoan on Crete, Helladic on mainland, and Cycladic on islands)
Mycaenaen	1400 - 1100 BC (contemporary with late pre-Hellenic)
Archaic	800 - 500 BC
Classical	500 - 300 BC
Hellenistic	300 - 146 BC
Greco-Roman	146 BC - 330 AD
Byzantine	330 - 1204 AD

171

Greek Terms, connected with Archaeology

Acropolis — highest point of city with the principal buildings
Agora — market or meeting place
Asclepeion — sanctuary of Asclepeios the Healer
Amphora — vessel for storing wine or oil
Caryatid — column in the shape of a clothed female figure
Enceinte — precinct or area
Entablature — area between the columns and the pediment of a temple
Exedra — semi-circular bench
Frourio — fortress
Hephaisteion — temple of the Fire God Hephaistos
Heraion — temple or sanctuary of the Goddess Hera
Heroon — shrine of a Hero or demi-God
Hieron — sanctuary
Iconostasis — screen separating the main part of a church from the
          altar, into which icons or holy pictures are set
Kastro — castle or fortress
Khora — place, usually the principal place in an area
Kore — girl or statue of a girl (archaic)
Kouros — boy or statue of a youth (archaic)
Krater — urn shaped storage vessel
Larnax — burial vessel, usually of terracotta (plur. larnaces)
Madrassah — Moslem theological school or college
Moni — monastery or nunnery
Nymphaeum — monumental fountain (of the nymphs)
Odeion — recital hall, shaped like a theatre but usually covered
Pantokrator — the Christian God or all-Creator, usually depicted in
          mosaic or fresco in the dome or apse of a church
Plateia — village or town square
Propylaia — sanctuary entrance or gateway
Stela — gravestone, usually with relief carvings (plur. stelae)
Stoa — free-standing portico of colonnaded walkway
Stylobate — temple floor
Tholos — circular tomb (pur. tholoi)
Votive — statue or other object placed in a tomb.

Index

173